Serving with Popski's Private Army

Revised Edition 2025

Popski's Private Army

This small company lived and fought many miles behind the enemy lines, in the scrub of the desert, and in the mountains and plains of Italy, pitting their courage and wits against great odds.

Their feats as varied as their methods, but they all had one single aim—the harassment of the enemy by all physical and moral means.

Sunday Chronicle July 10th, 1949.

Chapter 1

I joined the army in September 1939, at the start of World War Two at the age of twenty-one. First the Royal Engineers, Pioneer Corps, part of the B.E.F. in France; a spell on the Isle of Man, military training, and guarding the internees in the camps, then followed the K.S.L.I. and six months spent in London training to be a Signalman in the Royal Corps of Signals.

June 27th, 1943. I was on the first ship in the convoy to disembark at the docks in Algiers, North Africa. Infantry regiments, Royal Engineers with their bailey bridges, Service Corps with their Lorries, Royal Corps of Signals with their mobile transmitters. Tanks and armoured vehicles were being unloaded from the last few ships by the 76th Tank Corps. Ordered to form three ranks, according to the regiments we were in, we marched through the town of Algiers, to the outskirts of a racecourse and turned into an army camp.

The following day there were trains waiting with empty goods wagons to take the infantry to Philippeville, where we found all the Service

Corps scattered about in a cork forest. All the infantry regiments joined them.

The enemy had been surrendering to the First and Eighth Armies since May, and the army stretched from Cairo to Algiers.

With the North African campaign now ending, the desert war was virtually over. Eighth Army began to plan its part in the invasion of Sicily. One evening my mates and I were handed passes; we decided to go to the Kasbah. We all got drunk on the local wine and, after returning to camp, I got my head down in the tent. As I was drifting off to sleep, I was half aware of one of my two blankets sliding off me and disappearing below the small gap where the tent met the floor. I dashed outside; no one there and no sign of the blanket. Turned out a few of the other lads had a blanket missing next morning too.

A couple of days later, for a small amount of money, I bought my blanket back, (either mine or somebody else's) in the form of a warm coat, from the Arab who had whipped it, and that coat saw me through many a cold day in the mountains of Italy later on.

July 1st, I became ill with malaria and went into a field hospital in Philippeville. On July 10th – 50th Div. – and 51st Highland Div. of Eighth Army landed troops in Sicily in a combined British-American-Canadian invasion, with amphibious and airborne landings at the Gulf of Gela and North of Syracuse. They immediately captured Syracuse, then swept up the East coast into the Catania plain, and crossed the river Simeto, where they found the enemy in considerable strength on the Mount Etna line. In Sicily, Catania had fallen to the allies. The Americans had captured Ranzzazo on August 12th. Eighth Army took Messina from the South, with Americans from the West. The Germans, having not been able to prevent the capture of the island had removed most of their troops to the mainland, the last leaving in mid-August.

It was on September 3rd that the Eighth Army crossed the Straits of Messina, landing on the toe of Italy. Central and northern Italy was now largely occupied by German forces.

The disillusionment of the Italian people against Mussolini reached its peak in July, 1943. Mussolini was dismissed by Victor Emmanuel

III and Badoglio was appointed as premier; the Fascist Party was disbanded. Italy surrendered unconditionally to the Allies, and declared war on Germany.

News came through that the Italian government had surrendered in September; the Italian people, I think, had never been keen about their participation in the war. Nevertheless, the German forces were ready to fight without their help. Forces from the U.S. Fifth Army landed against heavy enemy resistance at Salerno; British forces at Taranto captured Bari, and airfields around Foggia, mainly in the West at the port of Naples, almost unopposed, under cover of allied aircraft operating from Sicily.

I was hospitalized again for a couple of weeks in October 1943, after suffering a relapse of malaria, and November 1st, I was discharged from the hospital and sent to a re-enforcement camp for displaced soldiers. Many soldiers waited to return to their regiments or to join another regiment.

It was during this time that I became friends with a young wireless operator named Howard Sloan: everyone called him Toddy; he was 21 years old. The two of us were eager to join our unit, the 50th Division, or at least another unit. An announcement was posted on the notice board one morning, asking wireless operators to report to the camp commander. There were about eight of us who went along.

'A major will interview you tomorrow,' the commander told us.

The next morning, Major Peniakoff arrived. He was a man in his mid-forties, about five feet nine inches, and heavily built. He wore a black Tank Corps beret. The insignia on it was a small silver badge in the form of an Astrolabe. It turned out to be more of an interrogation than an interview. At the end of the interview, he inquired as to how I had acquired my knowledge of German. I replied that I had worked in Switzerland prior to the war.

After reviewing my pay book, he asked a few more questions, and the interview was concluded. Towards the end of the day, the camp commander informed Toddy and I that we were to join Major Peniakoff's unit, actually it was on the notice board too, and that the major would send two of his men to pick us up the following morning. toddy was also able to speak German, and I wondered whether this had played a role in the major's decision.

We packed our kitbags.

'Do you know what regiment we are joining'? I asked of Toddy.

'You know as much as me,' he answered.

The following afternoon, at 14h00, our names were called, saying our transport was here.

What looked like a couple of brigands had just arrived at the camp in an American jeep; neither was wearing full uniform and both looked a bit scruffy. The short, stocky, unshaven bloke, who wore rimless glasses, jumped out of the jeep and confidently strolled into the commander's office. A minute later, the camp commander came out with him and pointed to us.

'Those are your men.'

He glanced over at us. 'Are you the two ops? Throw your bags in and jump on,' he called.

Toddy and I climbed into the back of the jeep and sat on our kitbags. The driver, who had stayed in the jeep, had a black patch over one eye, and this, along with a scarred face, gave him a sinister appearance.

During the journey, neither of them spoke to Toddy or me, just occasionally to each other.

Curious to know where we were heading, I leaned forward. 'What regiment are we joining?' I asked.

Still staring straight ahead, the driver answered, 'You'll see when we arrive; our orders are not to divulge any information.'

So, I kept quiet and began to wonder what I had got myself into. We arrived at our destination: Sfax. The driver said, 'Get your bags. I will go and see if the major will see you.' Whilst Toddy and I waited, we learned our driver's name was Al Locke, it was said of French origin, aged about 26; the short, stocky bloke was Charles Curtis, nicknamed 'Bum', aged 24, a mines and demolition expert. 'The major will see you both now, leave your kitbags there,' said Locke.

Major Peniakoff was sitting on a wooden bench inside the tent he used as an office.

'Come in, lads, and sit down,' he said. He asked us our names again.

'Howard Sloan, Sir,' he turned to me.

'Leslie White, Sir.'

'The squad won't have any trouble remembering your name, you'll be nicknamed Chalky' he said. He went on.

'I will give you some information about us. My unit, PPA, is a Special Service unit. I am forming a new squadron, which will consist of three operating patrols, six jeeps to a patrol, two men to a jeep, plus a forward HQ patrol, known as Blitz, under the command of Captain Jean Caneri. We will be operating mainly behind enemy lines, and the aim of the unit will be to collect intelligence, inflict damage on the enemy and, therefore, spread unease. However, our service can be tedious too; the attributes we require are endurance and a steady nerve and, if a patrol gets Into difficulty, we all help. I have known heroic men in battle, and yet, they could not stand the pressure of our operations. If either of you feel this type of service is not in your line, speak up now.'

The major went quiet to give us a moment to consider. Both Toddy and I remained silent and he carried on. 'One jeep in each patrol will be fitted with a transmitter/receiver; whichever patrol each of you is allocated to, this will be your jeep. There will be a 50 browning which you will have to practice firing as you will be wireless op/gunner. Your driver will be responsible for all mines and explosives. The same with the other jeeps, the driver's partner will be gunner and use a mortar. First and foremost, you are the hub of your patrol; your work is most important, as information will come through you. I cannot impress upon you more, your knowledge on the transmitter can save lives and I expect every man in PPA to get to know those in their patrol and respect one another. I have handed back most of the lads I had In Africa to their regiments of origin, and my new unit will be mostly new recruits. We are all brothers here; there is no saluting of ranks, the NCOs who join us are required to give up their ranks, and promotions in the patrols are re-earned. We have two trucks here, one a store, one a weaponry. You will be issued with an automatic pistol and have the opportunity to practice pistol firing, that is one of my rules: you must never be without it. After you leave here, go to the stores. They will fit you out. Go to the armoury truck for your arms. You will be taken on probation; if, at any time, either of you are found to be unsuitable you will be R T U d – returned to your unit. On the other hand, if a man wishes to leave, he would be allowed to do so and returned at the earliest opportunity.

'Right,' he said, standing up, 'That's just about everything, any questions?'

Toddy and I stood up to attention. 'No, Sir,' I answered.

'No, Sir,' Toddy repeated.

'The two lads who brought you here were part of B patrol in Africa; they are leaving for Italy to join their patrol which is already in Italy looking for possible sites for a temporary HQ for the unit. We will be here whilst the adjustments are made to our new jeeps. In that time, you can become acquainted with the lads and use of the gunnery.' The major finished by advising us his men call him Popski.

Toddy and I were now members of 'Popski's Private Army'.

Major Vladimir Peniakoff (Popski)

Chapter 2

Toddy and I, became acquainted with some of the other newly recruited men; some having dropped their ranks they were Pte. Burrows, Pte Cokes, Sgmn. Franklin, and Wilson, Spr. Mc Allister, Pte. Ben Owen, Sgmn. Stan Steward, and Gnr. Walker.

Popski, born in Belgium of Russian parents; was a highly intelligent man, educated privately and at Cambridge, England. He could speak English, French, Russian, Italian, Arabic German and Dutch fluently. Over time, I came to respect and admire him enormously.

Word came through the jeeps, which were being modified at R E M E at Trani was ready. The following day Popski, Toddy, I and the other new recruits (some had already left for Italy) – went to the port, where we embarked the LCT's (landing craft, tank) The place was full of Italian and German prisoners of war being put on to ships going to Canadian POW camps.

We were taken to Syracuse, in Sicily, by the S.A.S. My first sight on landing at Syracuse was a dead donkey lying on the road covered with maggots, and sadly, rows of graves with makeshift crosses along the roadside; many were marked '50 Div.'

Having camped for the night, we continued along the winding road to Taormina, which was unaffected by the fighting and pulled into the square. In a nearby park, we pitched our tents and made camp. It was a beautiful location, and Mount Etna could be seen in the distance.

It was unclear why we had come here. There was a hotel at one side of the square, Eighth army HQ. Popski stayed at the hotel. My next step was to write to Alice with the new information regarding my unit and address. The letter was not likely to reach her until after Christmas.

Popski allowed us to go out in the evenings and we went for a drink. I met a local lad who was a barber; he told me that German officers had been in the hotel for a long time— right up until our troops landed; then they had quickly left. He was so happy the Germans had been routed he asked me if any of the lads wanted a free haircut. A few of the lads took him up on his offer. Later he asked Toddy and me if we would like to meet his parents, who lived some way away. I told him we couldn't, as we had orders to stay within the vicinity of the camp. One afternoon I was walking back to the camp, when a Sicilian man stopped me; he had his wife and baby with him. He pulled out a knife and said he would finish me off if I didn't give him whatever money I had, saying he wanted to buy milk for their child. It was true: the people had very little food to eat and there were plenty of muggings going on. The authorities had found a number of dead soldiers in the canal. I had very little money on me, so I advised him to go and get help from A.M.G.O.T. (Allied military government in occupied territories) He was becoming more agitated, and pointed the knife directly at me, seemingly ready to lunge forward. I was about to draw my pistol to warn him off when, just at that moment, a couple of passing British soldiers saw what was happening and ran towards us. The man, with his wife carrying the baby, ran off. I decided to take a shortcut through a courtyard back to camp. As I walked along, I noticed a small silver spoon lying on the ground. I thought that would do for me; my own spoon was not very good, as it was only aluminium, attached to a fork and knife, not very functional. I bent down to pick up the spoon. As I started to lift it, it seemed heavy. I then remembered an incident from a few days before, when a soldier had used a lavatory that had been booby-trapped. When he pulled the chain to flush, an explosion killed him. A young Italian boy picking grapes from a vine in a vineyard, he too was killed.

Still holding the spoon, I noticed a cord attached to it, buried in the dust. I felt the blood drain from my face and a cold chill ran through me as I realized it was a booby trap. Carefully, I laid the spoon down again and marked the spot, for it to be removed.

We were informed by Popski that General Montgomery would give a speech at the nearby amphitheatre, Teatro Greco. It was mandatory for the 50th Div and 51st Highland to attend; not so Toddy and I as we were now in PPA, but we went anyway.

Monty told the lads in his speech that he would be taking them back to England. It was to be for training for the D day landings in France; this was not disclosed to the men at the time. Many booed him. There had been great loss of life in Sicily. Afterwards talking with the lads of

50 Div. I was told they had had a bet with lads from 51st Div. as to which division would be the first to plant the Union Jack on the peak of Mount Etna. I hoped it would be my old div 50, turned out to be 51st Highland.

Popski informed us we would be leaving at 15h00 the next day. Consequently, we gathered our equipment, ensuring everything was in order.

The following day Popski emerged from the hotel with a bundle of maps and papers in his hands, signalling the start of the journey to Messina. As we drove along, I was struck by the devastation, there wasn't a single standing house in sight; instead, all I could see was rubble. Sadly, again we passed many graves of the lads I had come with overseas; the markers served as a reminder of the sacrifices made by those who had gone before. At the waterside were members of the S.A.S. We drove onto LCTs which transported us to a nearby island to pick up dry rations and ammunition from the Eighth Army stores located there.

After staying overnight, with the necessary supplies in tow, we embarked the next day and made for the Messina Straits and Brindisi, in

Italy. After we arrived in Brindisi, one of the patrol leaders, in a US jeep, Captain Bob Yunnie, skipper of B Patrol arrived with Captain Jean Caneri – known to the men as Jan met us; and guided us to Bisceglie, to meet up with the other PPA men. Most newly recruited. We drove up a dry riverbed and the unit assembled together– W/Lt. Bray, A.H. Tpr Hughes, N. Tpr. Hardman, S. Tpr. Coupe, I. Tpr. Davis, W. Gnr. Summerfield, R. Pte. Hodgson, D. Pte O'Leary, W. Pte. Dunham, T. Pte. Moss, H. Pte. Wilson. W. Spr. McAllister, J. Gnr. Walker, A. Pte. Owen, B.J. Pte. Burrows, E. Pte Cokes, R.H. Sgmn. Franklin, A.J. Sgmn. Sloan, H. Sgmn White, L.R. Sgmn. Wilson, A.H. Sgmn. Steward, H.S. W/Lt. Bray, A.H. Tpr Hughes, N. Tpr. Hardman. Tpr. Coupe, I. Tpr. Davis, W. Gnr. Summerfield, R. Pte. Hodgson, D. Pte O'Leary, W. Pte. Dunham, T. Pte. Moss, H. Pte. Wilson, W. If

Capt. Jean Caneri (Jan)

there were others, their name eludes me at the moment. A good proportion of the men in the patrols were from the S.A.S, Commandos and Para's, and NCOs who had dropped their ranks on joining.

Over time more men would be recruited and also leave. We moved into our billets, seven villas on the Adriatic coast, situated between Bari and Barletta, near the town of Bisceglie. Popski made promotions, of some of the men who had come through the deserts of Tunisia and Libya with him. SQMS. McDonough, J. appointed (SSM). Cpl. Curtis, C. & Cpl. Sanders, E. appointed Sgts. Pte. Moss, H. Dvr. McDonald, G. L/c. Beautyman, J. L.c. Brook, E. Dvr. Mitchell, R. Tpr. Riches, F. appointed Cpls. Spr. Porter, D. appointed L.Cpl.

Popski told the wireless operators to go to HQ wireless station, which was a black American 15 cwt. Dodge truck, and introduce ourselves to Cpls. Eric Brooks and Ted Beautyman who were in charge of the signal section.

'Eric will put you at your ease and inform you of the procedures we use and anything else you want to know,' he said.

It was nearing Christmas day, Popski arranged a lunch with free beer for the lads, in Bisceglie; we all signed each other's menu card.

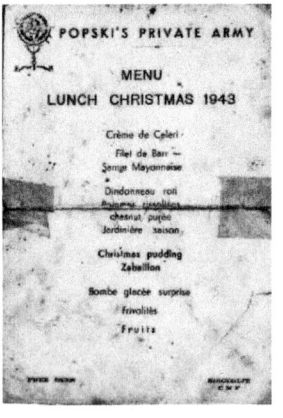

On Christmas day, Ben Owen (now assigned to B patrol) and Al Locke went down to the beach to catch fish for lunch; many of us went down too in the jeeps. Ben and Al each took a grenade, pulled out the pin and threw the grenade into the sea. Hundreds of fish came floating to the top. We filled the jeeps with the fish and then brought them back to the villa we used as a cookhouse. Our Russian cooks, Ivan and Nikolai, were busy chopping wood, and speedily set about preparing Christmas dinner for us all. Afterwards, as I relaxed in the most comfortable chair I could find, I closed my eyes and thought of Alice, my wife back home. I wondered what she was doing at that moment—probably eating Christmas lunch at her mum and dad's house, with the whole family there. I hoped she was thinking of me, as I was of her.

I thought, too, of lovely Heidi in Switzerland, the girl I was to marry before I was forced to leave the country owing to the imminent threat of war. I wondered if she had found a new young man to fall in love with her; I thought of dear cousin Elsie and her husband George— Elsie had joined the A.T.S. and was at Barnard Castle operating the Anti-aircraft guns. I hoped Elsie was still safe and, with all my heart, I wished all the best for each of them …

Field Marshall Kesselring, the German army group commander in southern Italy, had been given command of the whole of Italy and ordered a series of defensive lines South of Rome. Lt-Gen Sir Oliver Leece took over Eighth Army from General Montgomery.

By the end of December, PPA was fully equipped and ready to begin training the new personnel. Popski appointed Captain Ricky

Rickwood skipper of P patrol, Stan Steward Wireless operator. 2/Lt. Reeve-Walker was appointed skipper of the newly formed S patrol, Sgmn. Franklin wireless operator. Sgmn. Wilson was appointed wireless operator to B patrol and I, wireless operator in HQ Blitz, with adjutant Captain Jean Caneri.

On January 1st, 1944. Popski headed to Naples to arrange the unit's transfer to 10 Corps, and in preparation for ski patrols he hired three Italian ski instructors. A relapse of malaria caused Popski to be admitted to the hospital at Caserta the following day. We were inoculated for TAB, tetanus, and typhoid on the 9th.

The Fifth Army, which consisted of American, British and some French Moroccan troops had moved up from Naples, they were held back by the Germans at Garigliano and Cassino, preventing them from continuing their advance. Capt. Caneri, adjutant, reported to the commanding officer in Caserta on January 11th. PPA was transferred to 10 Corps, under the command of the 5th Div. Popski returned from a ten-day hospital stay on the 12th, and he, along with Jean Caneri, reported to 10 Corps at Saliense and Fifth Division at Casanova where administration and a new location for the unit were found.

Popski drove over to GHQ, Caserta for orders for the patrols. An Anglo-American force was to sail further up the coast; land by sea and carry out a solid beachhead build up; the patrols were to play a part in the first wave.

Capt. Yunnie of B patrol and Sgmn Cpl. Beautyman were given orders to leave Bisceglie on the 13th in W/T truck and report to CO at Casonova. Following Popski's order, P and B patrols under command of Captain Rickwood pitched camp in an olive grove near Casonova, followed two days later by 2/Lt. Reeve-Walker with S patrol and Capt. Caneri and Lt. Bray with battle HQ.

On the 17th, at Carano, the patrols were all set for the drive to Naples to embark, the Garigliano battle was to begin that night. Then Popski received a signal from HQ, they had cancelled our part in the landings. The force sailed without our unit and landed on the beaches near Anzio and Nettuno at dawn, relatively unopposed. German reaction to the landing was swift, and months later, the force was still battling with the enemy in the coastal areas.

It was about this time, there were further promotions in the patrols. Beautyman to Sergeant, and Bill O'Leary to Corporal.

The Garigliano front was static, there were no jobs for PPA on the horizon. So, some days later when Popski was asked by the General at HQ to provide a foot party of men to blow up a single-span masonry bridge at the river Capo Daqua, 1000 yards behind German lines, north of a village named Minturno—Popski agreed. The general had said that it was essential, as the bridge was the only way the enemy could infiltrate into British lines; also, blowing the bridge would have a demoralizing effect on German troops. B patrol was the most experienced at this time, some of its members having been on operations in Africa.

After conducting a survey of the area with Popski, Capt. Bob Yunnie thought it a pointless operation as the bridge could be bypassed with another bridge nearby. Still, the mission was to go ahead despite this observation. Capt. Yunnie chose the men from his B patrol to carry out the operation. Bum Curtis (Sgt) mines and explosive expert, with his understudy, Paddy Mc Allister recruited the same time as Toddy and I. Ben Owen and Al Locke, ex-commando, Jimmy Hunter ex S.A.S.

Capt. Yunnie and his men departed early evening on the 31st, from the Scots guards' position and reached the plain of the river Capo Di'Acqua. After setting off from the mouth of the valley, the party encountered an S minefield, which tragically resulted in the death of Pte. Hunter. McAllister was severely wounded, Al Locke and Ben Owen slightly wounded, and therefore Capt. Yunnie decided that they should return carrying the wounded since the job could no longer be completed; the journey proving impossible before they had travelled a quarter of the way. Capt. Yunnie decided to stop with the three wounded and dispatch Sgt. Curtis to report to Popski, who was just below the Scots Guard position.

Bum reported to Popski shortly after 9 o'clock. Capt. Caneri and Cpl. Cameron, along with a shielding company of the Scots Guards, went forward to bring back the wounded. The operation was completed under heavy mortar fire in the early hours of the morning. It was the talk of the camp, and upon hearing the news, I was of the opinion that if they had taken a wireless operator and radioed the forward troops for assistance, they would have gotten help and away quicker. I learned many years later from Ben Owen that they had taken a wireless op, Sgmn. Wilson.

Al Locke recovered and returned some months later, but didn't remain long; he was sent to Egypt. Paddy McAllister recovered; and returned still weak. Eventually, Ben Owen recovered and returned from hospital to B patrol.

Chapter 3

Early February, the rear HQ at Casonova and the battle HQ at Carano, the patrols anticipated their assignments. Capt. Yunnie's B patrol was reformed, and Howard Sloan (Toddy) was appointed wireless operator.

Popski was interviewing and recruiting more members at 1 C.R.U. He took on strength eight drivers, Wilkinson, Hewitt, Galloway, Watkins, Croskerry, Saunders, Parkinson, and Alexander. Gnr. Rutherford, Gnr. Norman, Pte. Gale, Pte A. White, Haley, Beck, Cale, Hughes, Farrell, Rogers, and Sgmn. Mc Culloch, and training began under the supervision of Lt. Reeve-Walker. Popski was hospitalized and Staff Sergeant Mc Donough was discharged.

In order to test the new members of B patrol, a training scheme was conducted on the 12th in the Potenza area. The purpose of this exercise was to assess the men's proficiency. Next day, Capt. Rickwood took his patrol out to Mondragone to run trials of a road watch, to see how quickly information could be sent of enemy traffic, from a patrol to Division HQ, via wireless link of Ted and Brooksy in HQ wireless station. The wireless station was in the 15 cwt Dodge truck.

At Cassino, some 40 miles north of us, there was a Benedictine monastery. It was built in the 6th century in order to safeguard the route to Rome, and located on a hilltop at a height of approximately 1700 feet. The walls were 150 feet high and 10 feet thick. The German military, Spandau teams and bomb squads, were positioned on the hill below the monastery's walls and were able to observe the movements of Allied troops for miles. There had been bitter fighting and a heavy casualty rate, especially for the Allies since January, as they had attempted to move forward. Rumours and talk abounded that the German military was housed in the monastery itself, and so after great deliberation by the Allied commanders, it was reluctantly agreed that bombing the monastery was the only way for the Allies to advance. Popski was one of those who had been opposed to it.

The decision was made to launch an air attack; and we watched as waves of flying fortresses obliterated the area and Nazi paratroopers moved into the rubble and ruins.

Having spent a couple of weeks in the hospital, Popski was discharged, and Capt. Caneri was sent to No. 2 CRU (Serra Capriola) to interview officers who had volunteered for PPA.

P, B, and Lt. Reeve-Walker's S patrol on the 24th took part in a week-long training W/T exercise, so as to determine how many of the patrols could be commanded via HQ wireless station. SSM Mc Donough in charge of the heavy section, re-supplied our patrols with food rations, petrol, and ammunition.

PPA men were in and out of the hospital at this time for various reasons, and Popski decided to return men with VD to their unit in order to assist with the Anti-VD programme.

March 5th, at Casonova, PPA reverted to command of 10 corps from Fifth Div. A week later, the unit relocated to Caivano 3 district, Naples.

There was a flourishing black market at Naples, where anything and everything was stolen and traded. As a result of the prevalence of Typhus and lice infestations in the city, the U.S. army set up DDT dusting stations throughout the city, and U. S. soldiers doused the population, which was the cause of the Typhus outbreak.

In mid-March, the Allies launched another heavy aerial bombardment of Cassino, still without a breakthrough; and then Mount Vesuvius erupted, and the army used trucks to help evacuate part of the hospital and people living in villages on the hillside to Naples.
The unit was sent for further ski training, we were billeted in a hotel atop Peidimonte di Alife, in the San Gregorio area; which at the top of a nearly vertical, three-thousand-foot-high mountainside in the Matese Mountains. Divided into two groups, for a ten-day period we trained under the supervision of the unit's Italian instructors, Lt. Falcoz, Pte. Alliaud, and Cpl. Major Geraldini.
Men found to be unsuitable were being RTU'd. More men taken on, Pte. Cahill, Tpr. Sonley, Griffin, Hellier. Also, some time before, a young Captain, John Campbell, who assisted adjutant Jan Caneri.
Following the completion of ski training, Popski ordered the patrols to remain in the Peidimonte, San Gregorio area, and with a hundred square miles of Matese mountains around us, we were to conduct intensive

training in mountaineering, fake raids, blowing up unreal targets, and forced marches.

It was bitterly cold in the mountains; I wore the coat that the Arab had made for me from an old army blanket in Algiers. After dark, we were driven out and left in pairs between fifty and seventy miles from our base, several miles apart, carrying our weapons and packs containing a white square piece of silk material with a map of Italy on it, a small supply of food, a pencil which when snapped in half, was a compass, a few thousand lire in the collars of our shirts, and a garrotte in case of an emergency—our mission, to make our way back, across country with as little delay as possible, avoiding highways and habitat. We used live ammunition while learning machine gunnery; each man expected to be a driver, gunner, sniper, armaments observer, use a

L to R. Les (Chalky) with PPA driver (unnamed) and Sgmn. Douglas Mc Culloch.

mortar or bazooka. Then, as the weather warmed up a little, we moved from the hotel to tents in the park.

Little notice was taken of deportment, or uniform, and discipline was relaxed, but if a man disobeyed an order, neglected his weapons or jeep, or was sloppy whilst out on operations, it was punished by RTU (returned to unit).
April, in Caivano, Capt. Yunnie who had been hospitalized was discharged, and Hellier and Liles were admitted.

Jan gave up his adjutant job, and Lt. Hoar was appointed in the post. Tpr. Hubbard from the Lancers joined the unit; later in the campaign it was he who drove the only jeep to house a flamethrower; how many times it was used, I cannot say, I personally witnessed it being used only once.

Prior to the war, Jan Caneri had been employed in the legal profession and was exceptionally proficient in administration, (and scrounging for anything the unit needed), and with his intelligence and cunning, he had acquired a 399 mobile wireless station from district headquarters AQMG, for the unit. There were only a limited number of these sets and only army headquarters and above had them. In the wake of Brooksy's recent hospitalization, I was asked to man the wireless station with Beautyman who was promoted to sergeant and in charge of the Signal Section. It was vital that the wireless operators could operate the transmitter when Ted or Brooksy were absent. I found the new mobile 399 transmitter was not very different from those we used on the jeeps, just more powerful and could reach a greater distance.

The patrols were still in the Peidimonte area, undergoing intensive training, and men found unsuitable for Special Service were being RTU'd. At Acerra, Popski returned from the General hospital and he took 14 more men on strength. Some time back, Popski had decided to set up a mountain base at San Gregorio, supply it by air and operate from there without bringing the patrols back to our lines for refits, support, stores, and equipment. Popski told the officer who commanded troop movements he would be moving the unit HQ forward from Acerra to San Gregorio to establish a headquarters there, and would keep in touch by wireless.

I was with Brooksy working on the transmitter in the dodge truck. Cpl. Eric Brooks, a thirty-five-year-old Londoner, kept the truck locked, and kept the key to himself. No one was permitted to enter unless he invited them. Brooksy communicated to the patrols that HQ was relocating to San Gregorio, reporting first to the 12th Lancers. The Lancers were to accompany us en route and we arrived at their forward line where we camped for the night. On the map, Popski and Jan noted the isolated village of San Gregorio. I had just completed my shift in the wireless truck. It was dark, so I nipped out to the field for a pee before going to bed. I returned to find Popski standing in front of me. His usually good-humoured face revealed that there was something amiss. 'Chalky, where's your gun?' He asked annoyed.

I should have been carrying my pistol; I hadn't taken it with me.

'I could have been the enemy, and shot you. I have got rid of men because of this,' he said, and paused. 'Anyhow, wireless operators are hard to come by. Don't let it happen again' he said.

Popski allowed a man one mistake only. After this, I made sure I always carried my pistol. Popski and Jan went on ahead with B patrol. A message came through from Toddy. Popski's orders were the rest of us should follow.

The Germans had blown the two road bridges to San Gregorio, and access was by goat track or funicular. We used the funicular to take up the jeeps, which belonged to a hydro-electric plant and could carry two jeeps at a time. The last to go up on the funicular was the wireless truck.

In the small park, we pitched our lean-to tents, which attached to the jeeps, pegging the other end to the ground. I opened up a tin of rations and warmed it up, putting it in one half of my Dixie and threw the camouflage net over the jeep, then I sat with the lads whilst we ate our meal. It was late when I laid down my groundsheet and blanket in the tent and got my head down, wondering what tomorrow would bring.

S patrol was assigned to guard the perimeter of the camp, since word may have reached the enemy that we were here. Popski's headquarters was the hotel in the village. He commandeered the village council's property, where he conducted meetings with patrol leaders. Popski instructed Jan to arrange a meeting with the local village police. The police came to our headquarters, where Jan inquired if there were fascists in the village. He also asked to see the village priest, as he wanted information from him. Jan delegated the responsibility of our security to the police, requiring anyone leaving the village to report to the police when departing and returning.

Popski recruited five additional signalmen, increasing the strength of our personnel and whilst awaiting orders from Eighth Army, the men continued with training, i.e. driving the jeeps over tough terrain, and their maintenance. We covered the whole of southern Italy during our exercises, driving from map reference to map reference, as communicated wirelessly by Brooksy at HQ. There was no windscreen on the jeeps, and the guns were mounted on a swivel, with a fifty Browning belt-fed at the front, firing armour-piercing and incendiary ammunition, and a thirty Browning at the rear which provided additional support and protection against pursuing threats. We were taught how to dismantle and reassemble the guns until we were able to do so with our eyes closed, these mounted guns were to provide crucial defence and attack capabilities during future missions, allowing the patrols to engage enemy forces effectively.

Troops with all their armour were pouring in everywhere. At Cassino, the Allies, after savage fighting for months had made a push forward. The German soldiers who weren't killed fought amongst the rubble of the monastery and Polish troops entered Cassino, the last German soldiers eventually coming out of their fox holes, shell-shocked after being bombed day and night, were rounded up and became prisoners of war. There was a huge loss of life at Cassino, mostly amongst the Allies, and the whole area smelled of death for miles. The Anzio force emerged from a beachhead that it had been fighting since January 18th. The Adolf Hitler line across the Liri valley was attacked by the Seaforth Highlanders of Canada, as part of 2nd Brigade 1st Canadian infantry division and broken three days later supported by the tanks of the North Irish Horse, with the Polish Corps to their right, along with French troops on the left.

I returned to base from exercises, I collected my mail and sat down to read the five letters that had accumulated for me, all from Alice.

I wrote to Alice…

1/6/44

2188109 Sig. L R White, No. 1 Demolition Squadron, Special Forces. PPA C.M.F.

My Darling Alice,

Here is your letter that I have promised ever since I wrote that last one to you. You know the circumstances that I am in, but as I promised, I always will make it my first job to write these few lines. As you say it is all we have to look forward too. Well, Darling, I received five letters this time when I arrived back, and am I pleased to hear that our little Pauline is coming along okay! I am hoping for the day I'll be back and see her running to meet me. Well, Darling, you asked in one letter if I still had my ring. If I lost that, I don't think I should like to go into action at all. I think that's what's keeping me safe out here; it's like a lucky charm. And I think that all the time I wear this, I will be safe. But as long as you and Pauline are okay, that's all that matters. So, look after yourselves, Darling, and I will try my best to do the same. As you might know by the wireless, things are a bit stiff out here now, but we'll pull through. The day I arrive in Rome I will go to the first shop and buy you and Pauline something and post it straight away to you – a bit optimistic, ah, but I know that no one can hold up a man as determined as me. Darling, I have to bring these few lines to an end, but however short my letters are, I love you more every time I write a letter to you. So, Darling, for the present, I'll say goodbye and God bless you and Pauline and keep you both safe.

Chapter 4

Rome fell on June 4th and the Fifth army pursued the Germans in a disorderly retreat beyond the Tiber and the Allies entered Pescara on the Adriatic on June 10th.

Popski assigned me to S patrol with Skipper, Lt. Anthony Reeve– Walker, Sammy (Sgt. Stanley Sizer) ex-Para's, Bill and Hodge (Cpl. Bill O'Leary, and Dennis Hodgson) Sid Hardman, Norman, Mc Caley (Alfred Cahill), Domenico (Derrick Storey) and others.

We had everything we needed in the jeeps, including ammunition, grenades, mines, and explosive charges. There was a small wooden box with a transmitter/receiver mounted on the left-hand rear side of my Jeep. A drop-down front; brackets attached on either side; the key was inserted into a groove on the lid. There were message pads and pencils beside the transmitter, and batteries were attached next to it.

There was to be a sea operation. Popski selected 30 men from the patrols, Capt. Ricky Rickwood. Lt. Reeves Walker, Sergeants Charles (Bum) Curtis, Mitchell, Sanders. Corporals

Cameron, Porter, Riches, O'Leary and Hodgson. L/Corporals Owen, Davies. Troopers Sonley, Hellier, Taylor, O'Neill, Griffin. Drivers Galloway, Mee, WB Wilson, W Wilson, Williamson. Pte. North. Cfr Spencer. Signalmen Mc Culloch, Steward, Reece, Summerfield, Toddy Sloan, and myself White. Just enough men to fill 12 jeeps and load them onto one LCT. Lt. Costello left for Eighth Army HQ as liaison officer on the 9th, and we set out the following day for Monopoli No 1. Special Forces HQ.

Lt. Reeve-Walker reported to the 5th Corps on the 12th as liaison officer, and made contact with the naval officer in charge. On Popski's orders, Yunnie, Dave Porter (Cpl), a mines and demolition expert and partisan Gino, as well as Quinto, a local partisan leader from the mountainous region of Cingoli; set out on the 12th as an advance party from Manfredonia in a naval ML (motor launch) for reconnaissance of the landing beach area for mines and exits. The patrols then drove to Manfredonia in the jeeps. The following day we concealed ourselves in a lemon grove. When Dave Porter returned, Popski was informed that all was well, that no mines were present, and that very few German vehicles were on the road. In accordance with Popski's plans, we would be escorted north by two naval vessels, an ML and a motor fishing vessel equipped with a Bofors gun, and we would observe radio silence until we landed. After dark, we loaded the 12 jeeps onto the LCT. A detachment of 9th Commandos accompanied us on board. We sailed throughout the night and I spent some time chatting with Bill O'Leary (Cpl) and McCulloch (Sgmn) of P Patrol. In favourable weather conditions, we arrived out of sight of land in the early hours of the morning. After breakfast, Popski briefed the patrol leaders and explained the mission to the men. Between 22h00 and 01h00, if it was safe to land our party of men, Yunnie would be on the beach south of the mouth of the Tenna River, flashing periodically the letter R with a red torch. If there is no signal from Yunnie that evening, we will put out to sea and try again the following night. According to Popski, our landing point would be sixty miles behind the German lines, and based on his latest information, a few German forces may be located inland, some military traffic may be travelling on the coast road, and there may be control posts along the road and guards on the bridges. Bob Yunnie will provide an update on this. Popski explained that after landing, the commandos would disembark and establish a beachhead where the Jeeps could be unloaded. He said that he intended to make contact with the partisans, establish a base in the mountains which would be supplied by air from which we would be able to operate as long as the conditions permitted. As necessary, we would move our base north, but we would always remain in the rear of the enemy. Popski briefed us on our objective, a mountain town named Cingoli. According to Popski's reconnaissance photographs, we could take a route that would take us sixty miles along a route where bridges were still (hopefully) intact. We had to memorize it, forty-four cross roads through four small towns. There was another route to memorize if the bridge over the Tenna, near Fermo, had been blown since photographs were taken. The maps were to be destroyed, we were to wear shirts similar to the Germans and travel with speed and rendezvous with partisans in the woods, northwest of Cingoli. We must clear the last major road by 05h00, anyone who loses their way will be RTU (returned to unit). If we meet opposition, we will fight our way through, finishing off the wounded as no prisoners should be taken. Popski provided us with the code name we must use and wished us luck. That evening the LCT made a slow run in. The dot-dash-dot of Yunnie and the red torch signal were spotted by Popski as we approached the shoreline. Then things started to go wrong. Suddenly, the LCT shuddered, we had hit a sandbar, we juddered over it into deeper water, the same thing happened again, then we beached with a jolt, the anchor was lowered, then the ramp went down. The commandos filed silently onto land and Popski gave the order to start up the jeep's engines. Capt. Yunnie came aboard to brief Popski and gave him some unwelcome news. Whilst we had been at sea, the situation had changed. The German army was now in retreat heading north from Cassino, troops in the village's, vehicles nose to tail littering the nearby coast road, and all the other roads all moving north. Gino Mifsud who had forged fascist papers, surreptitiously travelled the roads on a bicycle, confirmed to Popski this was his findings also. It was a hard pill for Popski to swallow. Popski concluded our small unit of men and 12 jeeps had little chance of reaching the mountains by dawn, and so, he cancelled the landing. The commandos returned onboard, the ramp was raised, the engines were started, and then another unfortunate occurrence— the LCT, commanded by the Navy, jarred on the sand bar. The LCT rocked and moved several yards out to sea, then jarred again and was stuck. The fishing vessel had left earlier and the ML escort standing out to sea was signalled but had also got stuck. All the while this was going on, we could see the stream of headlights from enemy vehicles, plainly seen as they moved along the coast road. Surely, nothing more could go wrong. Then it did, we heard an aircraft, one of ours. A flare was dropped and all around us was bathed in light, amazingly, we were not spotted, then bombs fell from our side and demolished a bridge several hundred yards away. Since the jeeps could not be unloaded on shore, Popski instructed the men to ready themselves and take escape rations; we would be making our way ashore in small groups, resting by day and walking by night until we reached our objective. At 02h00, the word went round the ML had freed itself—there was a change of plan—we were to be taken on board. Popski decided a party, on foot, consisting of wireless operator Sgmn. Toddy Sloan with a 32-suite wireless set, which looks like a small suitcase. Ben Owen, Danny O'Neil, Gino Mifsud, and Quinto, should go ashore with Capt. Yunnie, with orders to road watch and send back bombing targets for the RAF. Throughout the remainder of the night, the men, over one hundred including the commandos were evacuated to the escorting ML using a small dinghy and two floats. Small parties of commando's went first. As they neared the ML, one group carelessly capsized the dinghy and the crew of the ML had to rescue them; this caused a delay. As dawn broke, mostly PPA men were left. Popski told us to swim for it and for those who were not strong swimmers, which included my signalman mate Stan Steward (Sgt.); we took inner tubes off the jeeps tyres and inflated them. Meanwhile, Bum Curtis (Sgt) laid charges, and eventually the LCT and jeeps we abandoned and destroyed. Less than a mile separated the coast road from the beach, and a railway line ran between them. An armoured train could be seen approaching from the distance. The ML skipper brought the train to an abrupt standstill with the Bofors, and the RAF was signalled to finish the job.

We arrived back at Manfredonia, Jean Caneri sent 15 cwt. trucks to transport us back to our base at San Gregorio; and over the following few days from the 16th, road watching was conducted by Yunnie's party. Toddy transmitted bombing targets from their location east of Fermo in the Tenna Valley to Brooksy and Ted Beautyman at our wireless station at San Gregorio. These messages were relayed to our station at 8th Army and received by Lt. Costello who rang up Desert Air Force— the bombers did the rest.

On the 19th, Popski with the main party of 10 jeeps left San Gregorio and headed north overland, to harass the Germans in their disordered withdrawal. Blitz was led by Popski with Cpl. Cameron driver, Sgts. Mitchell and Beautyman, and Sgmn Mc Culloch. S patrol with skipper Lt. Reeve-Walker, L/Cpl. O' Leary, Troopers Hardman and Storey, Cfc

Seamer, Gnr. Norman, and myself Sgmn. White. B patrol led by Sgt. Curtis, Cpl. Riches, Cfn. Stewart and Dvr. Mee. P patrol, with skipper Capt. Rickwood, Lt. Falcose, Sgt. Sanders, Cpl. Porter L/C. Davies, Tpr. Taylor, Sgmn. Steward, and drivers Wilson and Williamson and Pte. Barnes in 15 cwt. supply truck.

On the 20th back at base, Captain Caneri, and drivers Cahill, Galloway, and Wilson departed for a parachute course. For us, as a result of mishaps with two vehicles left at R.E.M.E workshops, we found ourselves the next day in Teramo, the town that the German army had evacuated two days earlier and which was now being controlled by local partisans, who were still celebrating. The same at Ascoli, Sarnano, San Ginesio, now held by local partisans. The patrols were welcomed in jubilation by the local people.

Whilst we rested that evening, Popski found an Italian partisan who offered to send his men to conduct a reconnaissance of the road leading to Tolentino, since it had been reported that the town had been evacuated by the German military. On returning the partisans reported to

Popski 'all clear' and the partisan leader offered to guide us along the country roads to Tolentino. Our forward troops were over one hundred miles to our rear, when after midnight, on June 21st, Popski and the patrols with the intention of crossing the river Chienti and proceeding in the direction of Cingoli, were coming from the hills into the river valley at Paterno, when without warning a burst of automatic fire came from a farmhouse to our left. Popski's driver, Jock Cameron was shot. The patrols returned fire, and Ted Beautyman led the way into the farmhouse with our patrolmen, to clear it; killing two Germans, the rest ran off. A sniper's bullet had passed behind Popski and ricocheted, hitting Jock, and, falling from the jeep, Jock sadly died in Popski's arms. Our partisan guide who had guided us along the country roads had disappeared; we believed he had set up the ambush. There was a graveyard nearby; the gravedigger was burying his partisan son who had been killed the day before by the Germans. Popski arranged for Jock's burial, and with our Patrolmen and PPA partisans in attendance read the moving service himself.

Popski sent P and S patrols separately to recce fords across the Chienti, whilst he with Blitz recced westwards over the mountain range. S patrol recced areas from Tolentino to Abbadia di Fiastra and we found enemy rearguard positions holding the line at the Chienti river. The following day, Capt. Ricky Rickwood and P Patrol were resting on a grassy slope when one of the men carelessly discharged his gun under his arm, wounding Ricky in the stomach. He was taken to a hospital in Sarnano. Ricky's surgeon refused to accept payment for the bullet removal operation, but was grateful for some medical supplies. It was touch-and-go whether Ricky would survive over the next three days. Fortunately, he did and returned a few months later.

Popski instructed a signal to be sent to Yunnie via Jan at base to join us when his mission in the Tenna Valley was complete. Yunnie and the men of B patrol had performed excellent work in the Tenna Valley, sending bombing targets for the RAF under cover of darkness while hidden in wheat fields. As they returned from Fermo that evening after their many adventures in the Tenna Valley, they were riding in a captured German car.

Over the following days, a damaged jeep led Hardman, Storey, Seamer and Barnes to return to San Gregorio, also Lt. Falcose; and our camp moved to Loro Piceno. The patrols made contact with the Polish 15th Lancers at Mogliano, and the Italian C.I.L. Nembo division at Abbadia di Fiastra. At Morrovalle, both allied and enemy troops were present in large numbers.

Popski ordered Sgt. Sanders, now the skipper of P Patrol, and men in two jeeps to scout routes through the Sibillini mountains to Bolognola, with the objective of moving PPA south of Camerino in order to penetrate German lines, where no British troops were present. It took Sgt. Sanders and the men considerable effort and perseverance to reach the ridge of Monti Sibillini, which overlooked Bolognola, they reported to Popski that even if the jeeps were able to descend to Bolognola, there was no way to bring them back up. The following day, while B patrol departed to clear Calderola of enemy troops that then withdrew to Borgiano north of the river Chienti; Popski with Blitz and P patrol drove to the ridge and walked down to Bolognola with the small detachment of men. Bolognola to Polverina Valley was controlled by Brigada Sparsico, partisans, several hundred men commanded by Major Ferri, and his brother Guiseppe of Pisa University. The partisans comprised of local men, escaped POWs, refugees, and ex-Italian soldiers active in the area. They raided enemy traffic and destroyed railway lines and bridges, local people who lived in the Chienti valley, provided food for them. Popski learned that a division of German reserve troops was positioned and in control of the small town of Camerino, in the Apennines, close to the border of Umbria, between Potenza and Chienti valleys. A number of German attempts were made to capture and kill the partisans, but both the partisans and the locals fled into the woods. Upon their return, they found their houses looted and burned. Camerino was situated on an elevated plateau and bordered by thick stone walls; beyond the walls lay a forest. Popski proposed liberating Camerino to Major Ferri, who was more than willing to join forces with the patrols. Troopers Hellier, Sonley and Burrows came up from San

Gregorio in a repaired jeep to join us. Major Ferri provided transport, and accompanied Popski along the valley. Together they crossed the Chienti and spent most of the day reconnaissance of enemy positions north of Polverina to Colfiorito. Popski encountered the 12th Lancers while travelling to Colfiorito. Popski requested that Major Ferri send a detachment of his partisans to observe enemy positions continuously from their remote posts around Camerino, and instructed me to send a signal asking for supplies, guns, grenades, road mines, and ammunition to be sent to us for Major Ferri and his men. Nights were spent mining the rocky gorges of the Chienti with partisans, and teaching them specific PPA tactics for ambushing enemy supply convoys. Because German patrols lost vehicles and men, they stopped using the river road daily, and used only the road to the town's rear. PPA demolition and mines experts moved stealthily into the area one night and blew up the Potenza bridge several miles from the town, causing only a small amount of damage purposefully, and many local residents participated in the felling of trees and clearing of tracks through the surrounding woods. The German commander sent out foraging parties daily to steal pigs, cattle, and fowl from the fields. Having ordered Major Ferri's men to harass them, Popski intended for the German commander to believe it was all the work of the partisans; thus, when our men in jeeps attacked with their fifty brownings, this would shock and surprise the German commander. Popski didn't stop there, he ordered our wireless operators to send out the call signs of several of our armoured units, six sets sending out bogus signals up to three in one hour; due to our high-up position, our range was reduced and was insufficient to interfere with the Lancers' real communications. However, it gave the impression that they had moved up the coast and had overpowered their left flank. After dark, Popski had two zealous Nazi POWs that had been captured by the partisans, brought to him for interrogation. The first soldier was a waste of time, so Popski devised this ruse for when the second soldier was presented to him. Two of our wireless operators entered the room and, with the appearance of having just received a situation report from Eighth Army, marked the large map on the wall showing their forward positions from the coast inland to a line to the rear of the enemy in the town. Popski, after the pretence of being called away, the man was left in the room with a partisan guard for several minutes. This was long enough for him to observe the map. Upon his return, Popski pretended to be angry and threatened to take the POW and the other POW back to the 8th Army where they would be made to talk. That same night, after being marched into a room and locked in, he found a small unlocked window from which he could escape, and he fled through the woods under partisan fire, which, unbeknownst to him, was deliberately missing him as he fled. Popski waited one day for the division commander to digest the escaped soldier's news. Meanwhile, we signallers jammed his messages.

On the morning of the following day, two patrols of Jeeps were formed following Popski's instructions, and we drove along the tracks and positioned the Jeeps at a set distance apart around the walls. Upon Popski's signal, we opened fire with the powerful firepower of the fifty Browning guns and continued to fire as we moved rapidly and haphazardly into various positions. Popski's goal was to create the impression that an infantry brigade was attacking them, forcing the German commander to flee by the rear road.

All was quiet that evening, and as a result of Popski's belief that the Germans had left the town, he had the jeeps lined up, and led us in the direction of the town. We were mortared within seconds, and Popski positioned himself in the last jeep so that the smoke generator could be used to screen our escape, which was on his jeep alone. It seemed evident that his tactics had worked, since that night Popski learned that columns of trucks, staff cars, and marching troops were all heading north from the road at the rear, the patrols and partisans helped them speed up by opening up with the guns. Many were killed when they returned our fire, however, no members of PPA. A group of partisans entered the town, and Major Ferri, with Popski's assistance, oversaw the election of councillors to administer the town.

Popski ordered Lt. Reeve-Walker and S patrol to construct a ford across the Potenza River. After recruiting local labour, the working party was fired upon with some casualties. Following Popski's signal, the 12th Lancers arrived at Camerino several hours later. Together with the Lancers, under Popski's orders, the patrols travelled to Castelrainmondo where an enemy rearguard was engaged and fought off with local partisan involvement.

The jeeps were towed by bullocks to the far bank of the Potenza river, where Popski ordered the patrols to operate in the mountains, fifteen miles on each side of the watershed of the Apennines, the front from sea to sea, up to 30 miles. Our objective was to hunt down the enemy and harass them in every way that the native situation and our inventiveness would allow, so they would be able to offer less resistance to the Eighth and Fifth Armies.

Chapter 5

Unlike the coastal regions, the mountains had fewer enemy troops and sometimes only a very narrow goat trail connecting villages, requiring jeeps to cautiously navigate. PPA was the only allied force with support from partisans and flanked by armoured car regiments with whom we occasionally made contact. The patrols engaged enemy rearguards almost daily, sometimes intense and hard fought, and met with fierce resistance. However, the process of liberating the villages was not without its own set of challenges; there was a special concern for civilian safety in these operations, as the patrols often engaged in intense firefights with the enemy as the patrols fought to gain control. The patrols would road watch, we concealed ourselves near a main enemy supply route and carried out surveillance of the enemy traffic moving back and forth. We were issued Benzedrine tablets, so keeping awake at night was no problem, however many preferred not to take them.

Other wireless operators in the patrols and I would transmit the information to Brooksy; he, in turn, would transmit the message to Eighth Army who, in turn, rang up the RAF. The army commanders greatly appreciated this work, as we gave them enemy troop movements and bombing targets in the area.

At the allotted times when I called in to Brooksy at HQ, I tried not to be longer than fifteen minutes, being behind enemy lines, it was possible for the Germans to use their RDF equipment to locate us. After my last call of the day, at 9pm, I drove back to where we had camped, covered the jeep with the camouflage net and deciphered the messages I had received. By the time I was finished, the other lads were usually asleep, and I was glad to climb into my warm Alpine sleeping bag for the night. When we could, we slept in outhouses or barns, left a sentry on guard, and took the risk of a German patrol coming along.

On one occasion, as dusk approached, the patrol set up camp outside a village, close to a farm. Lt. Reeve-Walker instructed Cpls. Bill o' Leary and Dennis Hodgson to investigate the farm. As they crept closer, they didn't observe any movement. Reeve-Walker decided that we should wait until it was dark before contacting the occupants. As darkness fell, Bill and Hodge went ahead; if everything was okay, they would signal the rest of us 'all clear'. We waited for a sign, but it didn't come. Then both of them reappeared. Bill reported that he had spoken to the farmer, who pointed out a barn where German soldiers were sleeping. It was a German foot patrol.

The farmer said we could spend the night in the farmhouse and leave the jeeps where they were; we were asked to walk behind the haystacks to the back of the house, and he would let us in. Two members of the patrol were instructed by Reeve-Walker to camouflage the jeeps with nets and then alternate watching and sleeping throughout the night.

As the farmer and his wife would have to answer for the missing soldiers, there was no question that we would take the sleeping German soldiers. Consequently, we made our way to the farm, where we were met by the farmer's wife.

After following her into a small back room upstairs in the house, we found two beds and three mattresses on the floor. She and her husband had carried the mattresses into the room, ready for us to use. She said she would let us know when the foot patrol had left. We were all up early the following morning, the Germans had left at 5am, giving us the opportunity to escape undetected. The farmer's wife gave us bacon and eggs to take with us, explaining that she was anxious that we leave as well. After thanking her, we continued on our journey and stopped to cook breakfast on our small stove.

The Italian people who were not fascists were glad to see us. The farmhouses were mostly occupied by goodhearted women with their children, while many of the men had joined the partisans. While we were given shelter and food, they were glad to see us leave once we left, in case German foot patrols came along; since they couldn't risk being seen to be cooperating with the allied forces, as it was likely that they and their families would be shot.

In the following days, some of the following routes were taken to reconnoitre: On 3rd July, Capt. Yunnie and B patrol were given roaming commissions by Popski and travelled to Matelica. Popski with Blitz, S, and P patrols recced to Colcerasa where we engaged the enemy rearguard on the road between San Severino and Cingoli. The next day, we recced Colcerasa and Treia. While B patrol chased the enemy from Esanatoglia and were given a rapturous welcome by the local people. Under heavy artillery fire on the 5th, S patrol, coupled with Blitz and P patrol, engaged the enemy at Castel Sant' Angelo, without suffering any casualties. The following day, my patrol S, led by Lt. Reeve-Walker, recced the nearby castle of Castel San Pietro.

After spending several days at Esanatoglia, B patrol recced further north. During a joint reconnaissance with A squadron 12th Lancers at Matelica on the 7th, the patrol went forward to Collamato and Attiggio and came under heavy mortar fire. Trooper Danny O'Neill suffered injury when his jeep tumbled over the side of a mountain; Toddy, who was also in the jeep, sprung clear and escaped injury when the jeep fell.

During the next day's action at Castel San Pietro, S patrol on foot and P and Blitz patrols in jeeps attacked the German forces, killing two and capturing one POW; the enemy vacated the area that night. Patrols of S, P, and Blitz crossed the Apennine mountains on the 9th by way of Foligno and then proceeded to Pietralunga, which had been falsely reported as a liberated area by the Eighth Army. One platoon of the 4th Indian division was defending the position against a ferocious counterattack by the Germans.

During this same period, B patrol moved on to Serradica and engaged the enemy south of Cancelli, then crossed the country towards Gualdo Tadino, engaging enemy positions along the way. In accordance with Popski's orders, Eric Brooks informed B patrol that we would be joining them at Fossato di Vico, a few miles north of Gualdo Tadino.

Blitz, S, and P patrols got as far as Gualdo Tadino area where we met the 12th Lancers with four armoured cars. We saw a monastery and pulled up. Popski said 'The Germans have a habit of placing observation posts in them, we'd better explore.' It was true the elevated positions of the monasteries enabled an enemy occupying them to see some distance, radio their artillery, and shell our troops with precision.

S patrol was instructed by Popski to investigate. He said, 'We'll cover you if you're fired on.' The road up to the monastery had a winding course, we drove slowly, so the dust rising would not give us away and we waited and watched to see who entered and left.

A German officer and two wireless operators arrived in a staff car at 8 a.m. The wireless operators appeared to be relieved each morning by two others. After dropping the wireless ops the officer was driven away and S patrol stayed on watch for the rest of the day returning early next morning. In the back garden, a monk was working. Lt. Reeve-Walker decided to make contact. The monk walked from the garden to the house, and two of the lads, sprang on him; one placed a hand over his mouth and instructed him to keep quiet. He was shocked put stayed quiet as Reeve-Walker asked him in Italian where were the wireless operators, he pointed to the top of the building. Reeve-Walker told him to go inside, we followed. Once inside Reeve-Walker, Sammy (Sgt. Stanley Sizer) Bill and Hodge, Sid Hardman and I, with a walkie-talkie crept up to the large door and peered inside; a monk was kneeling at the altar, and Reeve-Walker crept up and whispered to him, 'Signor.' The monk turned around, and Reeve-Walker pressed his forefinger to his mouth, indicating 'Keep quiet, and stealthily moved towards him.

'Tedeschi qui?' *Are there Germans here?* Reeve-Walker asked.

The monk answered 'Si, tedeschi.'

'Dove' *Where?* Reeve-Walker asked.

The monk pointed to the stairs leading to the top of the building. Reeve-Walker instructed him to walk up to the door, knock, and enter. We followed the monk stealthily as he climbed the steps. Upon reaching the top, the monk followed instructions and the lads rushed in, taking the soldiers by surprise. As it was so far behind the front line, they were caught off guard.

Besides the wireless ops who were seated by the set, three other German soldiers were conversing nearby. In German, O' Leary shouted, 'Hands up!'

As Reeve-Walker and O'Leary disarmed the prisoners, we covered them with our Tommy guns. We then took the prisoners outside, where the remainder of the patrol was keeping watch. It was Reeve-Walker's intention to capture the officer and the two replacement wireless operators due any time shortly, so we prepared to waylay the relief. There were three jeeps parked just outside the monastery entrance, with the 50-browning pointing to the gateway and two other jeeps parked and camouflaged in the foliage further down the road.

When the staff car came in sight, Reeve-Walker was notified by walkie-talkie. The car pulled in the main gate and the two PPA jeeps pulled in behind it, encircling it completely. Reeve-Walker and Bill O' Leary, pointed Bren guns at the officer; and the wireless operators, all looking stunned, surrendered willingly. The officer and w/ops were disarmed by Bill and Hodge. Reeve-Walker, pleased that no shots had been fired, gave me a message to radio to P patrol for Popski that we had seven prisoners, including wireless operators, radios, and code books, and there were no casualties. Stan Steward P patrols w/op received the message, and Popski responded with the message 'Stay there, we will meet you.'

Within fifteen minutes Popski's P patrol arrived with the Lancers in armoured cars; the officer of the Lancers informed HQ to send troops to pick up the prisoners. As Popski looked at the map, he said to Reeve-Walker 'It's only a few miles from here to the Assisi monastery, you might want to inspect there as well, and when you have done that, we'll meet back at Gualdo.' On the roofs of the houses we passed, white crosses were displayed, symbolizing neutrality, which the Germans largely ignored.

Our jeeps climbed all the way to the monastery. As we were making too much dust, Bill advised us to slow down and hug the side of the road. As we approached the monastery, we entered a forecourt, a monk came out to speak with us, thinking we were Germans. After Reeve-Walker explained to them that we were British and asked if they were harbouring German troops. The monk replied, 'No. Come, I will take you to the Abbot.' Reeve-Walker instructed the lads in two jeeps. 'Stand by your guns in case we need them.' Reeve-Walker, Sammy, Bill, Hodge, Sid Hardman Norman and I with a walkie talkie went inside. The Abbot too at first sight thought we were Germans, he emphatically told us. 'German military are not present here; I am a friend of the English.' This was confirmed by a search of the monastery, which found no evidence of German military activity.

Reeve-Walker chatted with the Abbot and the monks gave us refreshments, afterwards pointing out the beautiful building architecture. A monk gave me a book written in English in a blue cover, containing information about the monastery before we left.

The patrols met up at Gualdo Tadino to rest the following day. Gigi Cardona, the Italian partisan serving in B patrol, was sent by Popski into Fabriano as an observer. Gigi reported to Popski the intelligence he had gathered. There was a strong garrison with artillery and a Jaeger division in the town, the main roads were all guarded, and situated in nearby villages were detached mortar posts. Popski informed us that the time was right to take a stab at liberating the town. Capt. Yunnie and B patrol in collaboration with 12th Lancers were operating in the area of Gubbio not far from Fabriano, engaging the enemy and creating diversionary tactics. I received a message from Toddy saying B patrol was being fired on and pinned down in a valley. I radioed Popski with B patrol's position, who messaged me back. 'Go and give assistance, and P patrol with 12th Lancers will come and give support'.

We could see where the mortars were firing from into the valley below, then we spotted the armoured cars of the 12th Lancers coming up the road. The commander said to Reeve-Walker 'They haven't seen us,' and so we all positioned our vehicles.

The Lancers were positioned further back, they fired first. Within minutes the air was full of gunfire then, when they stopped firing our patrol moved in with our fifty browning guns and B patrol was able to move out of the valley and also fire at the mortar crews. Lt. Reeve-Walker and my patrol S, headed for Fabriano. Another message came from Popski, 'Don't enter the town of Fabriano until the Lancers arrive, we will all go in together'.

The road to Fabriano wound over a steep hill. German sappers had dynamited the steepest mile, collapsing part of the hillside. In the railway tunnel under the hill, they had blown up goods trucks, and so, believing the blocked tunnel was impassable, they didn't bother guarding it and concentrated their defences elsewhere. Prior to joining the military, Reeve-Walker had worked as a mining engineer, he suggested using an oxyacetylene torch to cut up the mangled trucks. Popski agreed and nearby villages were searched, a torch and cylinders of gas were found in Nocera. Over the next couple of days, Reeve-Walker went hard at it making the pieces small enough to be removed. We tied tow ropes to the bumpers of the jeeps and dragged the parts out; some smaller pieces were carried out by local men who offered their labour. As dawn broke, two armoured cars of the Lancers advanced up the main road to Fabriano and began shelling. Believing they were being attacked from the south, the enemy in the town concentrated their machine guns on the armoured cars, whilst the jeeps of P and S patrols stealthily made our way through the tunnel to surprise the enemy. Two jeeps stopped where the junctions met to cover us in case any of the enemy came along, then the rest of us then moved with full speed straight into the main square, all gun's blazing. The air was full of gun fire; the German soldiers on the mortar posts were taken by surprise and were killed. Several German soldiers emerged from the houses and surrendered; we heard the roar of many engines as the remaining soldiers retreated. We were able to locate the German infantry headquarters quickly thanks to Gigi's intelligence. Within minutes of opening fire with our fifty and thirty Browning guns, the headquarters was completely engulfed in flames. The roar of vehicle engines could still be heard as the enemy fled the town, and by midday, the town was a ghost town and the relieved inhabitants came out of their houses to greet us, bringing us all sorts of things, wine, fruit, cakes, flowers. Reeve-Walker asked were there any Fascists. They shouted 'Fascista scappare' and S patrol went out to make sure the fleeing Germans were not still in the area. An armoured car regiment of the household cavalry arrived two days later to assume control. The patrols rested for a day. On the 15th, my patrol came across a German Garrison. In the ensuing firefight, 22 German soldiers were killed, and the barracks and ammunition dump, was blown up. The patrol recced north of Cingoli, B patrol entered Gubbio, and the following day, the patrols gathered at Gualdo Tadino. Following this, orders were received from the Eighth Army to withdraw. A rest period was then given for the men, Stan Steward and I visited friends we had made in Bisceglie, after a group of us first visited Rome. Meanwhile, re-equipment of the unit was arranged by Lt. John Campbell, the adjutant, and maintenance of vehicles, equipment, and reorganization of operations was carried out. Upon returning to San Gregorio, I reported to Brooksy, who informed me that I had been promoted and reclassified from B III to BII wireless operator.

The patrols. Fabriano. 'The relieved inhabitants came out of their houses into the streets to welcome us bringing all sorts of things wine, fruit, cakes and flowers'—Below right. Sgmn. Les (Chalky) White seated next to the box that housed the radio transmitter.

Chapter 6

In early August, Popski became ill and was admitted to a hospital in Rome. As a result, Jan took command of PPA. Jan informed us that we would be participating in a five-day parachute training course at No. 1 Para School, Special Forces, at Paradise Camp, near Brindisi. For lads like me, who had no parachute jumping experience, it was particularly necessary. There was no getting out of this course.

Arriving early in the morning, we were billeted in an airplane hangar. The training was provided by a Polish major. He instructed us that before jumping out of an aircraft, we should undergo some ground training. The school's equipment was basic; we trained on wooden scaffolding called swings to learn how to control parachute wavering. After jumping many times into the sand, we hung from beams in a hangar and practiced jumping from an empty Wellington bomber fuselage doorway on the ground. The Major taught us how to land, roll, and release the harness quickly, to avoid being dragged along by high winds, and how to collapse the chute by running to one side of the canopy, then gathering it up. He stated. 'As you approach the ground after jumping from the plane, you should pull down on the back straps attached to you, which will lower the chute. Release the straps as you approach the ground, and the chute will shoot up again, making the landing less heavy.' Well, that was the fun side of it…

The following day was our first actual jump. While I was not looking forward to it, I told myself if the others could do it, so could I. It was all made light of by the lads. Each of us received a parachute and the instructor instructed us to harness up. One lad joked that he wanted a big parachute, as he was a big lad. The instructor ensured that we all had our parachutes on correctly and we walked to the plane for our first jump.

Upon first sighting the aircraft, I thought, surely, we won't be going up in that. The aircraft was an old, dilapidated Italian Savoia Marchetti bomber with two decks, which had been captured on an African airfield. I didn't think it would be possible for it to rise above the ground. I was on the upper deck; the engine started up and went down the runway, luckily, I didn't know part of the tail had just fallen off. As the plane lifted, it barely skimmed the sea, then it turned around and crossed back over land.

'When the red light comes on, No. 1 stick all line up behind one another, as close as possible,' the instructor said. They did. A green light came on, he ordered 'Jump!' All No 1 stick jumped, one after the other, until all on the lower deck had jumped. Then it was our turn on the upper deck. We attached ourselves to the straps. I was second in line, but was glad I was not first man out because he got sight of terra firma. I stared at the back of the man in front of me. The green light came on 'Jump!' He went out. Then, once again, I heard the dreaded word 'Jump!' And felt a push on my back. Out I went through the small door space, then the others, one after the other, nearly on top of each other. I was floating down; I heard a voice shouting 'No 2, pull on your back straps'. I looked down; it was the voice of the instructor. It all came back to me, what we had been taught 'Guide yourself to the landing spot, put your arms to the back straps of the parachute'. I moved forward until I was over the landing place. Remembering the training, I pulled hard on both straps and released close to the ground. I had an easy landing on both feet, collapsed the chute by running past it, banged the release buckle, collected the chute and, with a feeling of both relief and euphoria, away I went. I had done it…Now I had just four more to do, two the next morning, and two nighttime jumps and then I would get my wings. The airplane hangar in which we slept was fully illuminated throughout the night. I must have been having a nightmare; I awoke to someone shouting, 'It was you, Chalky, you jumped in front of me'. In the morning, I was informed that, periodically, I had muttered, in my sleep, 'That wasn't me who jumped out of that plane; never in my life would I be able to do that'.

The next morning there was a further problem with the Savoia and the jumps were made in a Dakota. I completed the daytime jumps without any mishaps. The following day the old Savoia crash landed on the runway and they scrapped it. We boarded the Dakota for the night jumps. We followed the same procedure as for the day jumps, except that a small light on the ground guided us to the landing site. As it was early evening, I could just make out the ground below when I made my first jump. The second jump, however, occurred much later, and the light had become so dim that I couldn't see the ground at all. I landed with a thud, fortunately nothing was broken.

Our Polish major took us to the coast the following day, where we performed several more jumps over rough terrain to gain experience landing on rough ground. During one of these jumps, the wind carried a short, skinny man out to sea. A boat was dispatched to rescue him. He was fine. Each of the men who passed first class received their wings, a small blue and white parachute with wings attached, which we sewed onto our battledresses...

Between June and August, the Allies had advanced beyond Rome, closing in on the Gothic line. The Gothic line was a heavily fortified position, running south from La Spezia on the west coast to Pisa, passing through the Apennine mountain range between Florence and Bologna, and ending between Ravenna and

Pesaro which is just south of Rimini, on the Adriatic coast.

The Eighth Army reached the Arno line south of Florence on the 4th of August, and in the week following August 8th, troops were in the southern part of the city, and the enemy had vacated it by the following week; the German divisions continuing to blow up every bridge as they retreated through the central mountains to their positions along the Gothic Line.

PPA HQ was located at the castle of Solfagnano, near Perugia, and we returned there for re-equipment.

Popski was hospitalized and Jan took command of PPA and in accordance with his instructions from the Main Army, he reported to Brigadier Rodney at the 9th Armoured Brigade HQ on August 23rd at San Lorenzo.

It was decided PPA HQ should be at Fighille; and with our heavily armed Jeeps capable of criss-crossing the stony spine of mountain ranges; which were untracked and thick with mud, the patrols were to go into action in a fresh role in the central mountain sector on the line of attack to the Gothic line, forward reconnaissance ahead of a cavalry regiment or on its flanks—i.e. keep in contact with the enemy behind the lines at night, gather information required to provide critical military and topographical intelligence for the advancing main forces, and transmit this information by wireless to base. Capt. Yunnie's B patrol was to operate under the command of A squadron 12th lancers in the vicinity of San Giustino. Lt. Reeve-Walker and S, with 12th lancers B squadron, in the area of Badia, and P patrol with skipper Lt. Costello was to be in reserve at two hours' notice at base at Solfagnano.

Top pic. Leslie.
The patrols

It was dusk and my patrol, S, was travelling uphill in single file along a goat trail near San

Giustino, the trail was just wide enough for one jeep. A gun post was observed ahead in the distance. The enemy had the advantage of being in an elevated position, and following Lt. Reeve-Walker's instructions, I radioed back to Jan, and orders were issued not to attack it but to wait until backup arrived. However, Lt. Reeve-Walker elected not to wait, but to go it alone and silence the gun with the fifty browning. Sammy (Sgt. Sizer) and Bill (Cpl. O'Leary) tried to dissuade him, but couldn't, and so Bill offered to go with Lt. Reeve-Walker and he climbed into his jeep. As they drove up the track, the enemy spotted them and opened fire with the machine guns. The bullets struck the jeep with devastating force, and a piece of the jeep was torn off, flying through the air and slicing Reeve-Walker in the leg. The impact overturned the jeep and Bill took quick action; before the jeep rolled down the hillside, he managed to jump clear, and sustained minor injuries in the process. S patrol, opened fire with our 50 browning's on the enemy position and our concentrated gunfire silenced the machine guns, effectively neutralizing the threat. I radioed Jean Caneri, and one of the lads applied a tourniquet to Lt. Reeve-Walker's injury. Blitz patrol arrived and returned him to the Lancer regiment, where he was bandaged and transported to a field hospital by the Red Cross. Although he lived, we never saw him again. After this incident, there were several days of intense firefights with the enemy, then S patrol was recalled back to base to await a replacement for Lt. Reeve-Walker. In the meantime, Bill was in charge. Lt. John Campbell relinquished his position as adjutant, after being appointed the new skipper of S patrol. The Gothic line was 120.000 metres of barbed wire many miles of anti-tank ditches heavy gun emplacement i.e. a couple of thousand machine gun posts, 500 gun and mortar positions panther tank gun turrets all well bedded in. Therefore, the German divisions had the advantage over the British army, who were trying to push up the Adriatic Strada. Every time the British advanced, the Germans would open up with the guns. The

Sgt. Bill O' Leary

patrols' job was to silence as many of these guns as possible and the best way to do this was to get behind them, as the guns were facing south, but to do that, the villages had to be liberated. In one instance, we approached a village; all was quiet. Then a ghastly sight greeted us as we approached the main square. The families of partisans, women and children, were lying lifeless on the ground. It was a heartbreaking and sickening sight. After committing the heinous act, a hasty retreat had been made by the occupying forces from the village; they had fled the scene, leaving a trail of destruction in their wake. While contemplating the horror of what we witnessed, we heard a commotion in the distance; it was the partisans who had been fighting for their freedom and liberation who came rushing towards the main square. They took charge and we proceeded with our operations. A major allied offensive had commenced on August 25th and the Gothic Line defences were breached on both Eighth Army and Fifth Army fronts, west of Pesaro but without a breakthrough; and towards the end of August, PPA then passed under the command of 27th Lancers, Lt. Col. Horsburgh

Porter, and switched over on axis Citta di Castello, Apecchio, and Piobbico. S patrol and HQ Blitz patrol were based at Belvedere and B patrol together with C squadron collaborated in the liberation of Piobbico, and at end of August, a new HQ was established at Piano.
As time went on, Popski's original assignment of men to patrols changed, and men were assigned to other patrols. In addition, more men were added to strength due to death, injury, or RTU. Sometimes men who had served in the fighting patrols for some time, such as myself, were assigned to HQ Blitz patrol for a period of change or rest. Blitz at that time distributed supplies to patrols behind enemy lines, and were just as endangered.
Sant Angelo in Vado was entered by Capt. John Campbell's S patrol, then P patrol relieved B and S patrols and at the end of August whilst P patrol operated in Sant Angelo area, S and B patrols were in reserve and resting at Apecchio. Jean Caneri went to Rome to visit Popski. Capt. Yunnie became ill with malaria, and Capt. Ricky Rickwood returned. Because he was not fit enough to lead his patrol, he performed administrative duties.

Chapter 7

That week after Sept. 3rd, torrential rain fell and the Eighth Army and Allies penetrated a further ten miles of the Gothic Line along the Adriatic. The temperature in the mountains could drop below freezing at night, making it difficult to stay warm. Jean Caneri had some time before scavenged full-length flying suits for everyone from the Americans, which was very welcome. The men wore Alpine caps with a peak in the Middle and a mixture of British, American, and even Italian uniforms.

There was constant rain. Jean Caneri and Lt. Col. Porter decided that as Sant' Angelo area was not suitable for PPA operations, the patrols and HQ should move base to Urbania, and operate from Apecchio, the patrols to reconnoitre the enemy flank of the Gothic line between Lunano and Mercatale and the river Foglia.

PPA relocated its headquarters to Urbania and contacted the battalion of San Marco, which was scheduled to depart the next day. A single patrol was sufficient to operate in the area, which although challenging was more suitable for PPA operations. S patrol entered Sassocorvaro on foot on the 6th, which was empty, devoid of partisans, but heavily mined. On September 8th, Blitz, my patrol, was transporting supplies to B patrol. We reached a river; the enemy had blown the bridge. Due to the Germans' placement of mines around blown bridges, caution was necessary. The river had a ford, a shallow area, and Bum Curtis, our sergeant, cautiously led the way across, followed by Cpl. Ron Cokes.

I followed Ron with an 18 set on my back. While crossing the river, a sudden explosion occurred. Bum had stepped on an S mine that was hidden among the rubble; the water in the area was red from blood loss. The right leg of Bum appeared to be severed and the left leg was severely injured. Ron was injured on the backside. When I looked down, blood was oozing from my leg, but I was fortunate in that it was only fragments of shrapnel and small stones from the riverbed. I waded through the water, reached the riverbank, and sent a message to the partisans. The partisans came immediately. Jan Caneri and the others helped to bring Bum and Ron out of the river. Bum

Curtis was in a bad way; Jan managed to get a doctor, and we all went to an Italian hospital. There was only one doctor and a couple of nuns; all surgical instruments and just about everything else had been taken by the enemy, with only a few bandages remaining. As the doctor was unable to do much for Bum, he made him as comfortable as possible. Ron Cokes' wound was washed by the doctor and a nun, and a pad of cotton wool was applied to help stop the bleeding, the other nun washed and bandaged my leg. In the aftermath of this incident, I returned to the Lancers and went eventually back to my patrol. Ron was transported to a field hospital for treatment; he had sustained only a flesh wound and didn't suffer severe injuries. When he recovered, he returned to patrol duty.

Due to the heavy rain, S patrol was bogged down in mud between Peglio and Sassocorvaro. After crossing the river Foglia, the patrol entered Mercatale on foot, where heavy MG fire forced them to withdraw.

After crossing the same river, B patrol reached Lupaiolo without attracting the attention of the enemy and without being fired upon. However, shortly after a foot patrol of the 27th Lancers was ambushed, captured, and taken prisoner at the same location.

The patrols then received bad news. Sgt. Charles 'Bum' Curtis had sadly passed away at the casualty clearing station at Urbino; he was 25 years old...

Over the following days, Popski who had been hospitalized was discharged and took command, P patrol relieved B patrol, and B patrol occupied the village of Peglio to protect the town of Urbania. On September 15th, P and S patrols pulled out and returned to Solfagnano for a period of complete rest and to await the anticipated battle and big breakthrough at Rimini.

B patrol reported to 5 Corps 46th Div. 128 brigade headquarters at Trarive, their assignment to take part in the battle for San Marino. When they arrived, they found a patrol of Ghurkhas had been assigned in their place. B patrol was given a roving commission. After a heavy tank battle, San Marino was entered. After heavy fighting, Rimini was captured on September 21st by the Allies.

Popski sent Jean Caneri with P patrol along the front line to explore what possibility there was of breaking through into the plain. The Po plain was crisscrossed by rivers and canals, with some banks forty feet high. He arrived at Borgo San Lorenzo; the most promising prospects were in the American sector.

A couple of days after this at Borgo San Lorenzo Capt. Caneri drove to Fifth Army HQ in Florence the following day for a conference with generals Howard and Brann. The upshot of the meeting with the generals after analysing the battlefield conditions and considering various strategies to gain ground, they determined that the current line was guarded by a formidable, thickly held force, to have a chance of a break through using armed jeep patrols.

Jean Caneri and P patrol returned to San Angelo in Vado to reconnoitre area of Carpegna, while B patrol returned to Cattolica. Villa Grande was liberated by the patrols.

At the end of September, there was more heavy rain, swelling the rivers. Jean Caneri appointed Canadian Lt. George (Jigger) Lee as patrol commander in place of himself—and on

October 1st, P patrol liberated and entered Sant Agata, Feltria, and the following day joined S patrol at Perticara. S patrol carried out reconnaissance of Tornano and Masano and came under heavy fire whilst lifting mines at Savignano a few days later.

In the early hours of October 8th, P patrol returned to PPA HQ at Cattolica. B patrol was ordered to Sarsina to coordinate with Wheeler and Lynn Force. After reaching Citta Di Castello, they were held up by bad weather, and it was several days later when they reached Wheeler Force.

S patrol contacted Lynn Force and engaged the enemy at Monte Petra, then withdrew to Via Mercatino to rest.

During the second and third weeks of October, we were operating in the area of Civitella Di Romagna, local residents assisting greatly with intelligence gathering.

Early November, Popski and the patrol commanders reconnoitred the future operational area of PPA. Three patrols under the command of RCD Porter Force, although in reality, PPA was still led by Popski and was in charge of its own destiny; with responsibility for a section of the line extending from route 16 south of Ravenna to just north of the river Savio to the sea; a distance of approximately 3 miles.

A substantial amount of the area was flooded, woods crisscrossed by deep canalised rivers running between high banks. The coast was a sandy beach with low sand dunes. The enemy held the area mainly with secluded positions under the riverbanks, in farms, haystacks and sand dunes, all approaches covered by minefields; they had good mortar and artillery support.

Jan Caneri asked me if I would go with Brooksy for a while, Ted Beautyman had been pythoned back to England and only a handful of us could operate the wireless transmitter in the truck. The truck had a camouflage net over the top, and towed a generator behind. The truck, which Brooksy also used as an office we entered from steps at the rear. Running down the left-hand side was a table; Morse key attached. On the table the transmitter/receiver, had a vast range – it was on 24 hours a day, messages coming in from Eighth Army and the patrols. Codebook, pencils, pads and other stationery were also on

the table. A bench ran alongside the table, for
the operators to sit on. On the opposite side of
the truck was a large map of Italy, and several
area maps, so Brooksy could find the map
references for the patrols and troops in the area.
Below the maps – on the floor – was a bed. In
the corner was Brooksy's small personal radio,
which ran on an accumulator; the radio was
nearly always tuned in to the BBC. He kept the
sound turned down low, and the radio kept him
in touch with what was going on in England.
Working in the wireless truck was always very
busy, Brooksy and I alternated working on the
transmitter, while the other rested or slept, and
the BBC station on Eric Brook's radio was a
godsend, keeping us in touch with home. We
were not specifically listening for enemy
messages; however, it was sometimes possible
to pick up local radio stations and if you could
understand German – listen in.

Seaborne operations were contemplated, and
some days later when the weather improved
Popski and the patrols tried out and was
successful at loading our fully armed jeeps on to
DUKWs and the DUKWs onto LCTs. P patrol

began training with the jeeps in DUKWs in preparation for these amphibious operations. During a reconnaissance of Fosso Ghiaia, B and S patrols on foot encountered the enemy. Under heavy fire one of the partisans attached to the unit was wounded. For the following three days the patrols remained there maintaining standing and mortar positions. Meanwhile PPA moved base from Solfagnano to Viserba near Rimini. P patrol finished their DUKW training and after a few days rest at Savio, set out on an amphibious operation. On the 9th, the patrol landed on the beach along Fosso Ghiaia. The following day they took three German prisoners, one an officer, then Lt. Lee reported that his Sgt. Dave Porter, aged 22, and Trooper Tommy Croghan, aged 23, whilst laying mines across a ford so as to protect their position on the beach, had sadly both been killed.

Over the following days, Casa Delle Basse was set on fire with 50 calibre MG8s and attacked by B patrol and PPA partisans and occupied. P patrol relieved B patrol, and was heavily shelled and mortared.

The patrols B and S joined with 27th lancers and the village of Fosso di Ghiaia where the enemy was in strength, was forced into surrender by bringing in ten jeeps cloaked by the early morning mist, opening up at close range with twenty 50 Browning machine guns and flanked by the lancers who carried out fifteen minutes of shelling. On foot PPA and the lancers rushed the houses where the enemy was ensconced with the outcome of one enemy killed and two of our men wounded. Dick North of S patrol got a bullet in his hand; and Lt. Falcoz the Italian officer who originally came in January last, to PPA as a ski instructor was badly injured and had a foot blown off with a Schumine. The southern half of the Pineta Di Classe (pine forests in the Emilia Romagna delta) up to Fosso di Ghiaia a coastal belt between the Savio and Baveno rivers was cleared by a night landing of the jeeps, using D.U.W. Ks, capturing one German officer and two other ranks. Skipper, Capt. John Campbell, began a series of covert operations. Popski was persuaded by John that breakfast time was a suitable time for an assault, as soldiers were less alert at this time of day. S patrol whilst stationed at La Guaiadora learned there was a German post at a nearby farm named La Favorita. A partisan under the cover of selling them milk, for several days, learned of their routine and the condition i.e. minefields of the surrounding flooded area. The Germans remained alert throughout the night, however, they relaxed somewhat in the early morning and all but one went inside for breakfast. At dawn on November 14th, Capt. Campbell with Sammy (Sgt. Sizer) Bill and Hodge followed the partisan to the farm. They concealed themselves in a nearby barn for a brief period of time before racing forward. Bill quickly overpowered the sentry and dashed inside, only to discover five others still in bed or eating breakfast. The German soldiers finished their breakfast at La Guaiadora as P.O.W.s.

Chapter 8

Zucchenfico and Casa Castoniera were shelled on November 15th, and Cpl. Davies of P patrol and a partisan were badly wounded. Then the enemy blew the banks of the Fiumi Uniti River and flooded the area between the wood and Fiumi Uniti. The enemy now pushed back; a bridgehead made on the northern bank of the Fosso di Ghiaia. Under cover of trees, the Royal Engineers built a bridge Ponte Del Bottol over Fosso di Ghiaia and then Gorgo Fosso di Ghiaia was captured as well as the sugar factory in Classe by Riverforce.

The enemy, using mortar and artillery fire, was fierce, nevertheless, was being pushed back from the northern half of Pineta Di Classe up to the southern bank of the Fiumi Uniti, and forces cleared mines up to Ponte Nuovo. Outposts were captured, smashed, or fled. With the enemy under attack, there were just three posts guarded by German military on the south side of the bank of the Fiume Uniti, a wide river of rapid currents, no cover, and all bridges blown.

November 18th, Lt. Lee of P patrol was relieved of his command and replaced by a fit Capt. Ricky Rickwood, the patrol was renamed once again R patrol.

The following day Zucchenfico was taken, the result of information given by partisans. Popski's intentions were to, eventually, cross over the river and enter Ravenna. Since the capture of Classe and the Sugar factory, forces on the left flank of PPA had cleared the route up to Ponte Nuovo of mines. Meanwhile, on PPA segment of the line the patrols had the banks under surveillance and small arms fire. Popski sent out recce parties along the coast, north of the river mouth, to gather information about roads in the area and enemy defences.

A high medieval watchtower, the Caserma Dei Fiumi Uniti, was occupied by German soldiers at the mouth of the river. It was from here that they controlled a long stretch of coastline. The tower was shelled, but the stone walls ten feet thick prevented landings on the far bank of the river, where there was a road leading to Ravenna. John Campbell now nicknamed 'Bulldozer' after using his 'attack at dawn' methods, had been proven right on several occasions when this method, along with surprise, was used against outposts.

John told Popski he believed S patrol could capture the watchtower. Popski agreed to the operation with the condition that weapons must not be fired as this would alert the enemy.

I was assigned to S patrol for the assignment along with 14 others. We were dropped at night on the coast, approximately a mile from the tower. After reaching a cattle shed, approximately 30 yards from the tower, a 'watch' was carried out for a couple of days in order to observe their routine. It was crucial none of us made a sound; however, I had had a cough for a few days, which I tried to stifle, then the others nearly suffocated me in their resolve for us to remain undiscovered. Smoke began to come out of the chimney of the fort. John chose five men, which included Sammy, Bill, and Hodge to go with him to surprise the Germans guarding the outpost. He told the rest of us to

Capt. John Campbell. S patrol

wait nearby under the trees and 'be ready if this goes the wrong way'. At 7.30 am, a soldier with an Alsatian dog came out, the dog ran about and the soldier relieved himself. The lads held their breath thinking the dog would sniff us out, but he didn't and the soldier went back inside, shutting the heavy door. John and the other lads set off, wading through waist deep water to reach the tower. Luckily, they had not locked the heavy door and, typical of Bill and Hodge, they were off up the winding staircase, coming face to face with a German soldier with an automatic weapon. Bill floored him and the gun fell from the man's grasp, Bill ran straight to the top of the stairs kicked down a door; two soldiers were asleep in the room, another was sitting in a chair, cleaning a pistol. Before he could use it, Bill overpowered him and ordered them all to surrender which they did. Meanwhile, Capt. John Campbell and the others captured six German soldiers on the ground floor, all done to Popski's orders without firing a shot. We watched them come back splashing through the water with the prisoners who were put under guard. John told me to radio a code signal to Brooksy, who was in HQ truck not too far away, to say all went well and to ask Popski what we should do with the prisoners. At 11am, the German officer's orderly came along with a newly pressed coat for him, he entered the tower and was captured. Then another man came to look for the orderly, and met with the same fate. Popski arrived at 2 o' clock in DUKWs with R patrol, 27th Lancers and partisans, the partisans promptly took over the tower. A German patrol of four came to the fort looking for the others, and they too were captured. At 4pm, as it went dark, a larger patrol of eighteen, led by a captain, came along. There was a skirmish, and two German soldiers were killed, the rest, taken prisoner. Casa Sassi was captured, and all other posts along the coast were relinquished by the enemy.

In the afternoon of December 3rd, R patrol was set up at Baveno with an outpost of one officer and 35 men of the 27th lancers, (Cot Force) and ten PPA Partisans, at Caserma Fiumi Uniti. S patrol was relieved late afternoon at La Guaiadora and La Torrazza by partisans.

Just outside Ravenna, I rejoined Brooksy in the wireless truck. Canals ran through the low-lying ground where Brooksy and I were situated, and we were parked on a path that was just wide enough for the truck to pass through; the water was up to our waists if we stepped off the path. The enemy was mortaring the area, and they must have spotted us because they began firing mortar shells in the flooded area where we were parked. Diving under the truck, we sheltered from the mortars. A mortar dropped and exploded at the back of the truck, followed by another explosion at the front.

'We're being bracketed,' Brooksy shouted. 'The next one's for us.'

As we climbed back into the truck, Brooksy took the wheel and we began to drive away. Almost immediately, a shell exploded right where we had been parked.

Sgmn. Bill Cartwright who was now B patrols' operator messaged me saying there were indications of an imminent enemy withdrawal from Ravenna. December 4th, Ravenna fell to Canadian troops from the west, Porter Force from the south, 27th Lancers, 28th Garibaldi Brigade, and a PPA patrol, having crossed the south of Fiume Uniti river in DUKWs came ashore on the northern bank. The Royal Engineers built a jeep ferry over the river and two further patrols of PPA were overnight established in Ravenna.

Bill signalled me, Ravenna had been taken, and Popski wanted Brooksy and I to move up to the town centre. We wondered how we were going to get there, then decided to take a chance. Brooksy slowly drove through the water, between the telegraph poles either side of the road. It was like driving in a lake. Fortunately, the wheels found the bottom and eventually we made it. At Ravenna, the water had subsided somewhat, and the D.U.K.W.s were outside the Town Hall, where all the patrols were being feted by the dignitaries.

Popski gave us a glass of wine each and said, 'Come on in both of you and get something to eat'. There was a long table, with everything under the sun on it.

There is a beautiful old church at San Apollinaire in Classe, outside of Ravenna. It was believed by the army that the bell tower concealed an artillery observation post. Popski held off the shelling for 24 hours while he sent men to investigate. By disproving the rumour, his decision and swift action prevented an attack on the historic church.

On December 9th, Popski headed out to recce the area in a Jeep with Cpl. Charlie Burrows his PPA driver/gunner and partisan Gigi Cardona. The partisans were located in a wood nearby and a post of the Lancers, a handful of men with a Sergeant and a few Bren guns were on foot on the main road. I learned later that Popski had left Charlie with the jeep on the road, about 80 yards from a bridge, whilst he and Gigi went to check out another bridge guarded by the partisans; they had been patrolling the area and reported all was quiet. On returning to the jeep, Popski and Gigi were caught by surprise by a counterattack launched by the enemy on the far side of the canal. Under fire, they jumped into water in a nearby field which came up to their knees.

Popski, hit in the ear struggled back to the jeep to find Charlie sheltering from a hail of Bren gun fire. An elderly man coming up the road riding a donkey was hit and killed instantly. There was the sound of many more guns and the enemy began rushing over the bridge *en masse*. The rear of the jeep faced the bridge and Charlie jumped up and fired the 30 Browning. Several Lancers came running with a Bren gun, set it up and preceded to fire; under fire, their sergeant was killed. Gigi swivelled the 50 Browning and fired at the mass, hitting some; many others retreated over the bridge.

After a short pause, the enemy came running over the bridge once more, launching a second attack. Popski was hit in his left wrist, right hand and ear. Charlie fired into the mass again and the enemy launched a third attack, coming over the bridge and entrenching in large numbers on the side of the canal.

The first I heard of Popski's injury was when Toddy Sloan contacted Eric Brooks and I, we were just outside Ravenna, keeping in contact with H.Q. and all the patrols. Eric made a call to Jean Caneri who went to Popskis assistance. Charlie drove Popski to get medical help.

A troop of 27th Lancers with some partisans were trapped in a house nearby, overwhelmed, with little ammunition and several casualties, an attack was launched on the enemy position about a mile along the road, with two tanks of G.G.H.A leading, and Yunnie, with B patrol and Jean Caneri, following. S patrol was in reserve.

The tanks took up their firing positions and fired everything they had, with a huge reaction from the enemy. R patrol, with Capt. Rickwood, gave covering fire as Yunnie and B patrol kept the enemy busy at close quarters with the destructive firepower of twelve 50 and twelve 30 Browning's. Almost an hour had elapsed, when Don Galloway (Cpl) spotted a wounded lancer lying helpless and in danger of drowning in the marshes. While under heavy MG and mortar fire, Don ran to assist him, was wounded in the leg, but he still managed to carry him back to his jeep, within minutes it was all over, the wounded Lancers were evacuated. Don drove both himself and the wounded lancer to safety just before he fainted with loss of blood. There were 30 dead. B patrol was withdrawn and R patrol put in reserve. Don eventually recovered and came back to the patrol.

Charlie had driven Popski to a Canadian CCS where they operated and removed his left hand. I, along with others in the patrols, visited him. Popski was transferred to a general hospital in Rimini, and from there to another general hospital in Rome, and operated on again.

PPA patrolmen

B patrol was withdrawn and left Ravenna for base. Mid-December, S patrol alongside partisans established a post in the marshes NW of Porto Corsini. R patrol was relieved by S patrol. Capt. Campbell carried out a recce of Porto Corsini and decided it would need many men on the ground to take it. In late December the Lancers took over from S patrol in the marshes.

On December 18th, PPA passed from the command of 27th Lancers to Main Eighth army, and PPA and HQ and S patrol, we returned to base at Viserba. Jeeps were overhauled and men given leave, most visited Rome and Florence as did I.

For four months, the entire combat strength of the unit in the line engaged with the enemy on a daily basis, averaging 14 days in action, a few days for maintenance and refitting of jeeps, and then a couple of days for rest. By employing tactics that were suited to the local circumstances and conditions, PPA was successful in all operations through the use of surprise (no two actions were carried out in the same manner). The patrols of armed jeeps adapted to PPA prototype had been driven across country, mountain ranges, drawn by oxen over marshes, and through rivers. The mobility and enormous fire power of the jeeps was the key to the patrol's success. Popski fooled the enemy into believing they were up against a larger force than they actually were. PPA had had good assistance and backing from partisans and artillery. Royal Engineers built bridges and lifted mines under fire in forward positions.

Since early November PPA, operations to forward reconnoitre, gather intelligence, dislodge and the destruction of enemy rearguards, hold the line against enemy counterattack infiltration and enemy recce patrols; with never more than seventy men all told at any one time had had two men killed and seven wounded, had progressed eighteen miles against enemy opposition, liberated seventy-four square miles, captured forty-five prisoners, killed over sixty of the enemy, and fought many times its own strength. PPA casualties over this period were sadly two killed, seven wounded, partisans four killed, eight wounded.

Back at our new base near Rimini, operations stopped for the winter along the entire Italian front.

Lt. Gen. Mc Creery took over command of Eighth army, B patrols skipper Capt. Yunnie went home on leave at the end of December and the news came through Popski had been awarded the DSO.

More men were recruited by Popski—fresh faces were always coming and going, and there were more top-up vaccinations for us. On January 3rd, 1945, half of the unit's men attended a mines course conducted by Lt. Sands. The rest of the men attended three days later.

Eighth Army informed Popski that they had no

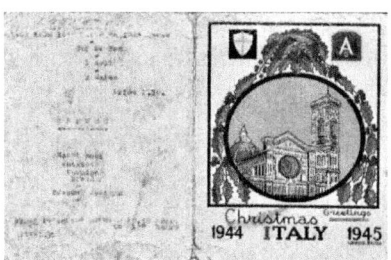
The menu from the patrols' Christmas dinner.

operations planned until battles resumed in March or April.

Popski scheduled a return to England in the middle of January, to have a hook fitted in place of the hand he had lost. Charlie Burrows, Popski's driver, and I, wireless operator, travelled with him to Rome. In Rome, Popski had friends, the Peroni family. They owned a brewery and provided him with a place to stay during his visit. Charlie and I stayed at the YMCA, where I met up with old friends from the KSLI. After a short stay, Popski's friends, the Peroni family drove him to Naples, and Popski sailed for Liverpool; Charlie and I headed back to base.

The unit moved to Montebuoni, near Florence, for training purposes and on the 25th Capt. Ricky Rickwood went home on LAIP. Jan Caneri devised many schemes and exercises to keep the men in peak fitness, similar to the training we carried out at San Gregorio. He sent new men for general training in weaponry and a parachute course to Brindisi. Every man had to be capable of being a gunner, a driver, member of a mortar or bazooka crew, artillery observer, sniper, commander of partisan detachment, skipper of DUWKS; plus, wireless operators could use four different types of special sets and two different cyphers.

By the end of February, under the direction of Capt. John Campbell, all the new men in the unit were trained, target practice, map reading, road watching, smoke laying, the lot, and were ready for action. In early March, Capt. Campbell was awarded the MC, and Sgt. Bill O' Leary the MM. In order to stop the men becoming restless and keep up morale Jan took over a hotel at a ski resort named Terminillo, in the mountains about fifty miles from Rome. Some 62 men were billeted in chalets. New men learned to ski, mountain warfare courses, climbing, etc. with time off for football, rugby, basketball and swimming under the direction of Lt. Wallbridge.

Terminillo

1.Gino Mifsud. 2.Frank Stott. 3.Nick Hubbard, 4. Don Galloway. 5.Harry Rose. 6.Bob Porter. 10. Howard (Toddy) Sloan. 12. Dougie Mc Culloch. 14. Ron Cokes. 15. Charlie Paine. 16. Dick North. 17. Paddy McAllister. 18. Jim Eastham. 19. Ron Jewell. 20. Jack Guest. 22 Ian Mc Callum. 23. Newman. 24. Eric Moreland. 25. Terry Duggan. 26. Eric Farr. 28. Arthur Rogers. 29. Les (Chalky) White. 31. Geoff Bays. 32. Ali Stewart. 33. D. (Alf) Davies. 34. George Sonley. 35. Victorio. 37. Summerfield. 38. Steve Wallbridge. 39. Barnes. 40. Rob Parkins. 41. Douglas Hellier. 42. Hector Simpson. 43. Bruno. Other men which may be in the photo. MC Closky. Garnett. Lt. Mc Cluman. Edgar Sanders. Les Kirby. Robert Parkinson.

***

Chapter 9

The men were given an additional weapon a sniper rifle. Another new weapon, affixed to one jeep in just one patrol, was a flamethrower… I myself saw the flamethrower used just once. This was one time when the patrols encountered an enemy barracks in the distance. As instructed, we lined up on a lane overlooking the barracks with the rear guns facing the barracks. A soldier emerged for a call of nature behind the bushes, and began walking towards us, which was unfortunate for him. To prevent him spotting us and giving away our position, the flamethrower was used to allow us to remain undetected. Following this, the order was given to open fire on the barracks. The enemy came out in force, bracketed and mortared us, and the last jeep was hit and destroyed. We had to get away quickly, and due to the absence of tarmacked roads, the air was dense with dust. Another time, not on this occasion, a mortar bomb dropped in my Jeep. It didn't explode, and I chucked it out quick. It was a dud.

In mid-March 1945, Jan, now Major Jean Caneri, attended daily meetings at the Main 8th Army with Lt. Colonels Smuts and Marling, Major Colquhoun, G.S.I.(Air) Major I.R.S. Crosby, N.L.O. Commander Whatley, No 1 Special Force Capt., Mc Dermott, O.S.S. Lt. Kelly, O.C. P.P. 2 Capt. Freeman and PPAs Capt. Campbell was re-called from the ski course, regarding PPA's participation in the forthcoming offensive—the unit was to stand by for operations as from 25th March.

The patrols returned to Montebuoni on April 3rd after ski training at Terminillo and on April 6th, at 6 am, B Patrol commanded by Capt. Yunnie and S Patrol commanded by Capt. John Campbell, each consisting of 4 Jeeps, fully equipped to PPA standard plus 2 Jeeps equipped with wireless sets B Mk. II and A Mk.III; in all a compliment of 2 officers and 30 men, sailed from Pesaro in RCLS to Porto Corsini, there to wait further movement orders. Days later, the Allied armies attacked after the winter pause with massive aerial and artillery bombardment, pushing the German line north west towards Bologna and began its spring offensive to cross the Po River.

Plans were afoot to land a party of PPA men in the area north of Lake Comacchio. However, Capt. Dickinson RN, stated the minefield approaches to the area were not negotiable under the hours of darkness. Storm boats that could have ridden the minefields could not take the weight of fully armed jeeps, and as there was no alternative to a landing by sea, the operation was cancelled; the patrols withdrew to Montebuoni.

Jan proposed an outlined plan for an operation to land six jeeps and eighteen men by glider in the Belluno area. Then Capt. Yunnie received tragic news from home in Scotland that his only son had passed away, and on the 11th, he returned home on compassionate grounds. Lt. Mc Callum became commander of B patrol. The patrols were in Cervia, squadron training, and on the 15th, Capt. Rickwood arrived from base to restart his duties as 2nd in command. My patrol was now HQ Blitz, an out and out fighting patrol led by Capt. Jan.

Jan visited Main HQ Eighth Army on the 18th, and Fifth Corps took over PPA. The following day, Jan headed again to Fifth Corps to discuss future operations. PPA was placed under the command of 56th Div, attached to 27th Lancers, and PPA patrols under Major Jan went into action along with the whole fighting strength of PPA.

Arriving early morning on the 21st, south east of Portomaggiore, the task was to give protection to the right flank of 27th lancers. The area between Dogato, Ostellato and Lake Comacchio was cleared by R patrol on the 22nd, capturing 22 German POWs. Based at Ostellato. R patrol made contact with the 28th Garibaldi Brigade and Marozzo, Lago Santo and Southern Codigoro was occupied. Strong enemy opposition encountered at Canale Volcano was encountered, in spite of this, 27 POWs were captured, including one officer. Migliaro and Massa Fiscaglia were occupied by S patrol, who built a wooden bridge over the Volcano Canal. By late afternoon, they had advanced just a few miles short of Iolanda Di Savoia, when the enemy withdrew. By mid-evening both S and R patrols were concentrated in Massa Fiscaglia with B patrol in reserve at 27 Lancer TAC HQ

The following day, after crossing the bridge at Massa Fiscaglia, R patrol occupied Mezzo Goro and reached the outskirts of Ariano Ferrarese, encountering heavy resistance, and taking 13 prisoners, including an officer.

S patrol crossed the Massa Fiscaglia bridge and occupied Iolanda di Savoia, engaging enemy positions two miles north of the town, capturing 25 POWs and wounding one. That day, several more engagements were conducted with the enemy before S patrol withdrew for the night to Massa Fiscaglia and the Italian Cremona Group relieved the patrols, taking over the entire area.

B patrol was assigned to reconnaissance a bridge south of Coccanile. At 2 o'clock, the patrol was ambushed at the entrance to a village. Lt. Mc Callum, the skipper of B patrol, leading in the first jeep, and his gunner, Spr. Mc Dowall, aged 24, were sadly both killed by a panzerfaust.

After a bitter battle that left several patrol men injured, Sgt. Don Galloway (who had recovered from his leg wound and returned to the unit) returned with the remaining patrol and 22 German prisoners to Blitz HQ, and Lt. Mc Cadell became the commander of B patrol.

Polish troops and Allied forces captured Bologna, and Ferrara fell. A large number of prisoners were taken.
Italian Partisans' Committee of Liberation declared a general uprising and crossed the river Po on the right flank of the Allies before making their way from northeast to Venice.
Jan estimated that there was nothing else that PPA could do at Ambrogio south of the river Po. As a result of a conference with TAC Army, Main Army, 5 Corps 56 Division, and SNOLE Ravenna, Jan Caneri with Blitz, patrols R, B and S, arrived at Porto Corsini an hour before midnight. Blitz with flamethrower Jeep, patrols, and jeeps, as well as stores, were loaded onto RCLs commanded by Lt. Brian Thomas, with minesweeper escort in preparation for departure on the 25th.
On the following morning, we set sail at six, with the RCLs flying the white ensign of the Royal Navy. Five hours later, four patrols of us veterans from Popskis No 1 Demolition Squadron arrived at the mouth of the river Po. Since local partisans occupied the area, the landing was unopposed. A fifteen-mile distance to the north was the Adige, and beyond that,

the Brenta. Lt. Thomas and his men would be attached to the unit from that day on, ferrying jeeps and men along the canals and lakes, plus taking back POWs, the wounded, and bringing up supplies.

Lt. Hearn USA OSS was to facilitate our operations for PPA and advancing Allied ground troops. Jan Caneri crossed the river Po on Friday 27th April with Blitz and B patrols. After encountering difficulties in their attempt to reach Rosalina via Mea, Lt. Wallbridge and R patrol crossed the Adige that evening at 6 o'clock. Several hundred yards north of the bridge, Jan Caneri with Blitz and B patrols encountered heavy artillery fire; therefore, we crossed at the same spot as R patrol half an hour later. The patrols spent the night at Caverzere.

S patrol travelled from Contarino to Donado Porto Levante to Loreo and made contact with Garibaldi partisans at Tornova. Having crossed the Adige at San Pietro di Caverzere mid-afternoon, they proceeded up the Gorzone Canale and engaged the enemy at Dolfina, capturing the bridge intact and taking forty POWs. Following the attack over the bridge, the enemy retreated and pursued over Canale di Cuole towards Cabianca, one officer and forty men surrendered. By mid-evening all enemy forces south of Gorzone Canale were cut off and had capitulated, supplies and materials taken in large quantities. The patrol returned to San Pietro di Caverzere, with 212 POWs who were evacuated in the RCLs along canals and lethal mine-strewn rivers, the mines being both secured and drifting. Lt. Steve Wallbridge and R patrol crossed the Brenta on the 28th. They were heading north-east towards Chioggia after crossing the Gorzone Canale at Dolfina. That afternoon, they came across Lt. Hearn and his small group of marines and partisans and Lt. Wallbridge learned the following. Lt. Hearn had heard rumours that the German garrison in Chioggia might surrender, and so he and his corporal, Rago, had set off for the town. After coming across an Italian fisherman, he had instructed him to go into the town, find a German officer, inform him that the US army was advancing, and that an American officer sought a meeting with him. Three German soldiers carrying white flags had appeared shortly after midday. Lt. Hearn had audaciously informed them that he had been sent to accept Chioggia's surrender and was invited to meet their commanding officers in the town at a hotel. As they sat at a table, Lt. Hearn through cheek and cunning convinced the 12 German officers that he had a regiment across the Brenta and an Air Corps was about to launch a devastating raid on Chioggia at any moment, and that further resistance would be futile, and that only a quick surrender would stop it. They appeared to believe his story. Lt. Hearn told them would be back at 2 o' clock to finalise details. As soon as he returned to his men, he had sent them in all directions in search of Popski's patrols. Lt. Hearn however, then informed Steve Wallbridge he felt doubtful the German officer would keep his word and would need further assurances. Lt. Wallbridge and Lt. Hearn returned to the town. Under a truce flag, they met the German commander who was reconsidering surrender. In no uncertain terms, Lt. Wallbridge stated that several battalions were just beyond the Brenta (there was only R Patrol and Lt. Hearn's men outside the town), and that they must surrender unconditionally within 24 hours or the Royal Air Force would

bomb them to smithereens. Following several hours of further bluffing by the two Lieutenants, the German commander now convinced, said that they were willing to surrender, as he believed their situation was hopeless. In response to a question regarding the number of civilians in the town, the German commander replied that there were three thousand seven hundred people. At 4 o'clock, they surrendered. The following day, B and R patrols entered Chioggia to disarm the garrison and found it consisted of approx. 700 men, one Field officer, 16 officers, ORs, 8 x 88 mm guns, 1 battery of coastal guns, countless 20 mm MGs, 15 armed barges, all port equipment, the electric plant intact, and supplies of food and ammunition for three months.
In Vigonovo near Padova (English name Padua, which I will use here), S patrol found the enemy firing four 88mm guns at our troops. On entering from the rear, Capt. John Campbell and S patrol charged and captured the guns, the predictors intact, and three trucks. A total of 300 POWs were handed over to the Partisans. After contacting the 12th Lancers at Camin, the

patrol entered Padua shortly after them, and returned to Chioggia shortly thereafter. Meanwhile, B patrol departed Cive early morning for Venice. The patrol engaged the enemy at Campagno Lupia, capturing 10 POWs and discovering seven suicides.

Local residents reported Dolo was empty of German military, however, when B patrol entered the town; around the square, they discovered the enemy barricaded in houses with approximately four coy in strength. The enemy fired at least ten Spandau's on the patrol and during the course of the fierce battle, Gunner Brown was wounded, and sadly, Arthur 'Spiv' Rogers aged 23 was killed. After forty minutes and almost out of ammunition, Sgt. Don Galloway carried a bazooka and fired three rockets at the enemy strongpoint and was wounded for a second time. The battle resulted in the village cleared, the capture of fifteen prisoners, the death

PPA patrols. Padua.

of seven others, and the patrol withdrew to Chioggia with the prisoners, wounded, and dead. Lt. George Sonway took command of the patrol.

On the 30th, the enemy was in strength at Iesolo. After sailing in the RCLs, R and B patrols took 31 prisoners, and 4 x 88 mm guns intact; and Popski returned and resumed command after a period of convalescence in England. The patrols returned to Chioggia for a period of rest, reorganization, and maintenance of their vehicles.

Partisans reported that after joining the German retreat towards the Alps, Mussolini and his mistress were captured and killed. Their bodies were now hanging upside down in Milan's Piazza Loreto. During this rest period, I witnessed the sight in Milan, along with other PPA members. In combat, I wrote Alice fewer letters; when I was able to write, I did, and I tried to keep

Popski and Ron Cokes

them cheerful. I knew she lived day-to-day, terrified she would receive a telegram one day announcing my death. I wrote…

2188109 Sig. L R White, No 1 Squadron, Special Forces, PPA CMF

My Darling Alice,

Just a line to cheer you up, which I hope will find you in the best of health. It's a week ago since I was able to sit down and write a few lines to you. I hope that you received them okay. Things here are the same war in the raw and it is raw. But there, I can't speak about it in a letter so that will have to wait till I can tell you personally, which I hope will be soon. How's our little Pauline getting on? I keep her photo always with me in my breast pocket and when things get bad, I just look at her and it brings back memories of long ago, which I hope will soon return. I suppose that the weather will just be getting a little bit better now, the weather here has broken and I think that within a couple of weeks we will have the usual hot Mediterranean weather; as long as it doesn't get too hot, I don't mind. But it's better than this blinking rain that we have been getting this last month or so. I can just imagine you shortly walking down the prom at Douglas, and wishing that I was with you. I suppose everything is as it was when I was there, not a lot of change. After the war, I think that we will settle down there in the good old IOM, what do you say? Well, I will have to end these few lines for now. Give Pauline a big kiss for me.

Chapter 10

It was Popski's desire at the beginning of the campaign, to enter Venice at the end of the war and lead a victory parade of his men and their jeeps around the Piazza San Marco square. Thus, it was to be.

At Chioggia, the jeeps were loaded onto three R.C.L s, with Lt. Thomas skipper in charge; I was in the second R C L. At daylight we set off, and sailed through the German mines between the island of St Giorgio and Venice— across the Grand Canal— entered the Canal San Marco, and moored the craft on the quay. The men piled onto the jeeps and, with Popski leading the way, we drove into the Piazzetta and turned into the Piazza San Marco, driving several times around the square. The delighted Venetian citizens in the square went wild, giving us a rousing and moving reception…

Blitz and the other patrols moved from Chioggia to Padua.

May 4th, as the war approached its end, German Army Group C, the axis forces in Italy, were retreating on all fronts. CQMS Davies was appointed B patrol commander; and Jean

PPA patrols, Piazza San Marco

Caneri returned to PPA HQ in Florence on python leave; taking with him the Italian personnel so they could go on leave, and some return to their homes.

A signal came through from Eighth army HQ with orders for PPA to report to Fifth Corps for further operations. The patrols left Padua for Udini.

At Udini PPA was placed under command of 6 brigade armoured Division and war correspondents interviewed Popski, keen to have the story of PPA.

In the early hours of May 6th, S and R patrols conducted reconnaissance parties in Gemona and Udini, Carporetto. They found the enemy withdrawing from Gemona. R Patrol reconnoitred the Udine Caporetto Road and contacted forward troops who were hampered by demolitions. PPA came under the command of the 61st Infantry Brigade.

The following day, after reporting to 61st Infantry Brigade HQ at six in the morning, Capt. Rickwood was informed that no jobs were currently available for PPA, since the 78 Division Recce Regiment had come into Tolmezzo from the west and had completed the tasks that were planned for PPA north of Tolmezzo.

It was an hour later that morning that Major Peniakoff met with Brigade Commander at TAC HQ Gemona to learn about the situation at Tolmezzo, and to conduct reconnaissance in two roads leading east from Resiutta and Raccolana. B Patrol reported road from Resiutta to Stolvizza was clear.

That evening, Capt. Campbell and S patrol returned from Tolmezzo to TAC HQ with information that 20,000 Cossacks were retiring north followed by 2 Squadrons of 78 Div. After travelling from Stretta to Acquafredda, Capt. Wallbridge and R Patrol entered Tarvisio at the request of the German commander, in order to protect a hospital from partisans. Capt.

Campbell and S patrol was sent to Tarvisio to join R patrol in the task.

Blitz and B patrols moved up to Chiusaforte. General Heinrich von Vietinghoff, who had taken command of Army Group C after Kesselring, had signed the surrender on behalf of the German armies. Brooksy gave Popski the news the war was over…

At dawn on May 8th, Blitz and B patrols moved out to join S and R patrols at Tarvisio.

At 8.35 a.m., the four patrols crossed the border between Italy and Austria with B squadron 27th Lancers, and proceeded to Velden, where Blitz and B Patrols remained.

In the course of their reconnaissance, S and R Patrols encountered the first elements of Tito's Army on roads from Velden to Rosegg, to Ledenitzen, Woroutz, St. Peter, and Weizelsdorf.

R Patrol returned to Velden.

S Patrol split into two groups. Instructions were given to establish good relations with Tito's forces, but to put up their hands if confronted. Capt. Campbell with the men in three jeeps travelled to Ferlach and Sgt. Sizer with three jeeps went to Eisenkappel.

PPA Convoy

Austria, near Villach. 1945

Yugoslavs enter Udine. 1945

German tank. Austrian frontier 1945

Popski.

German surrender

German soldiers inside Yugoslavia had been told by Yugoslav partisans that if they surrendered their arms, they would be able to enter Austria without fear of attack. Many of them did, and as a result, they killed them, and the Germans responded by killing them as well. Tito's Partisans fired upon Sgt. Sizer's party at Abtei, inflicting a wound on Albert (Chalky) White. A German Feldwebel, Sgt. Major, who was with a German group being rounded up as POWs, pursued the shooter, shot him, then returned and surrendered.

Popski reported to 5th Corps, and received orders to go to Graz the following day, in support of B Squadron, 27 Lancers and contact Soviet Forces. In the early morning hours, Popski and the patrols joined B Squadron 27 Lancers and travelled together along the route in the direction of Graz. As a result of three German divisions withdrawing disorderly before the Russians just beyond Wolfsberg, the roads were congested, and so progress was slow. Then we encountered hundreds of starving-looking men wearing striped pyjamas, heads shaven, and no shoes. Our convoy was stopped by Popski so that he could speak with some of them. They were Jewish and French political prisoners, just liberated by army officials from a German concentration camp near Klagenfurt. Whilst in the camps they had been deprived of food, clothing, and basic amenities and had been forced to make dugouts and barricades in working parties. To lift their spirits, Popski found a tricolour and encouraged them to sing the La Marseillaise, the French national anthem, which they did in weak, croaking voices. We arrived at the camp, there were many more skeletal men in pyjamas; Polish Jews used as labour parties for German forces, all now freed by the allies and being taken care of.

The Loibl Pass camp was a sub camp of the Mauthausen concentration camp, one of the most murderous. In 1943, 300 political Frenchmen The (resistants') were selected to dig across the Karawanken Mountains a tunnel between Austria and Yugoslavia.

In 1945 they were almost 1000 prisoners (540 Frenchmen). May 7th, the SS disappeared. The survivors quit the camp, walked through the tunnel to the north. May 8th, they met Tito's partisans and suddenly they saw the smoke of the British army vehicles! The leader, the man on the left, is Louis Balsan a great man, tank officer, he belonged to the Cartwright network created by the Intelligence Service. With the help of the British. They could now quit Austria. They were sent by trucks with Indian Sikhs drivers to Rome and Naples, and finally Marseille and Paris.

We neared Rosenthal village and contact was made with 5 Russian Tanks under command of Major Likov and Major Diemitshev; being the advance elements of the 84th Infantry Division (GOC Major-Gen. Buniashin) of 57th army 3rd Ukrainian front. Contact made and agreed that Russian forces should go to Voitsberg, and British forces to Rosenthal. Popski invited Major General Sergeiev and a few officers of the 61 Guards Division to breakfast the following morning.

At the Russians' request, a second breakfast was held; a conference was scheduled for later that afternoon, with the Russians' boundary being east of Rosenthal and the British boundary being west of Koflach; leaving a 2-kilometer zone free of occupation. The Unit moved back into Billets at Koflach. As a result of Popski's visit to Judenberg on the 11th, he and the Russian commander arranged for British troops to occupy Judenberg. The Russian troops retreated over the river Mur. Capt. Rickwood moved from Rosegg to Koflach while S patrol rested at Koflach. R Patrol travelled to Salzburg on the 12th in order to contact U.S. troops. Contact was made at Radstadt. After receiving reports that Himmler was in the area, R patrol went in search of him. In the meantime, Popski gave an interview to the BBC as well as the American War Correspondents in a broadcasting van.

To determine the details of the boundary lines, Popski, Capt. Rickwood, and Capt. Campbell attended a conference at Judenberg with Major Weir, the General Officer Commanding 78 Brigade and the Commander of the 30 Soviet Corps. The following day, word came that sadly, Albert (Chalky) White had died as a result of his wounds received at Udine. A second attempt to locate Himmler was made by Lt. Wallbridge with the assistance of three Jeeps from R Patrol and two Jeeps with men from S Patrol, who left Koflach for Radstadt at dawn. During this time, Popski and some of the members of B patrol travelled to Vienna via Graz, Bruck, and Weiner Neustadt, staying the night at Waldhoff. From Florence, Lt. Derrett established the PPA base at Rosegg. Meanwhile, Popski and some of the men from B patrol in two jeeps travelled to Vienna via Graz, Bruck, and Weiner Neustadt, spending the night at Waldhoff. Lt. Derrett established PPA base at Rosegg from Florence. The 16th. After failing to locate Himmler at Koflach, Lt. Wallbridge returned, and Popski returned from Vianne, where he was cheered by Russian troops. During our period of rest, a couple of football matches were organized. The first was against the Russians, which didn't take place, and the second was against the 27th lancers, which resulted in a victory for the lancers.

A report from base HQ came through, that an officer of PPA had accidently shot Cpl. Jimmy Snape in the stomach. Sadly, Jimmy's stomach wound led to his death a few days later. Capt. Ricky Rickwood conducted a court of inquiry.

Members of S. Patrol. Treppo Piccolo.
Top row far left. Les White (Chalky), Sammy Sizer, Norman.
Front row. L to R. Sid Hardman, Geoff Bays, Bill O' Leary and dog Louie, Danny Hodgson.

Louie joined S patrol after we came across a farm where he was half-starved and being beaten by the older son. He had kicked his eye out and some of the lads were inclined to do the same to him; however, Bill advised against this and offered the farmer one hundred cigarettes instead. The farmer did not hesitate, saying that he could always get another.

R patrol. 1945
A journalist took this pic for a newspaper article

As a result of further problems anticipated with the Yugoslavs on the Yugoslav border. Fifth Corps gave Popski instructions to send the unit to Rosegg as a corps reserve in case of trouble. In response to Popski's visit to Main HQ 8th Army on June 2nd, PPA was ordered to move to the military area near Montegnacco near Udine in order to be between the Army and the Partisans to the west. Capt. Caneri went on a 21-day leave, and Ricky Rickwood was given command of Blitz. Together with Blitz, B and R patrols moved to Treppo Piccolo, followed a few days later by S patrol.

Partisans were instructed to surrender their arms. Some did so, while others did not. The patrols received orders to begin policing duties from the 12th of June in order to disarm the partisans and prevent them from smuggling weapons that could threaten the peace. It was a dangerous job at times. Over twelve days, we set up checkpoints along main roads and bridges near Udine, where most of the partisans camped. Dignano, Tagliamento, Barcis, Via S. Pietro, la Delizia Latisana, Tolmezzo area, Somplago, Chiaicis and Rosegg. We were kept on our toes; however, the armed men took to the side roads. As a result of their policing duties, Toddy and Ben Owen experienced a narrow escape. Ben had returned to the unit a few days before the war ended in Europe following a six-month period in England, and they told us about it upon their return to base. As they sat in their jeep, hidden behind a tree on a side road north of Udini, a lorry passed by. Ben stepped into the roadway and extended his hand to signal them to stop. The driver drove directly at Ben with the intent of running him down, but missed him by just inches as Ben leapt into the ditch and avoided being hit. The three men in the cab cursed at Ben as the lorry roared past. After jumping into the jeep, Toddy fired the 30 Browning at the lorry, causing the rear tyre to explode. After swerving into a ditch, the vehicle overturned. When the local police arrived on scene, they discovered that the lorry contained weapons, ammunition, and contraband. Three men were inside the lorry and surrendered. The majority of the partisans were eventually disarmed and returned to their homes...

LIAP (Leave in Advance of Python) started a few days later, Sgt. Taylor and Tpr. Sid Hardman of S Patrol was the first to depart. The following day, Popski addressed the 16/5 Lancers on the same topic after delivering a lecture on the Russian Army to a battalion of the Grenadier Guards. The bridge and road checks were completed by the 24th, and a disarmament parade was held at Udine in the late afternoon for all Partisans east of Tagliamento.

Chapter 11

A chance to relax for a while. Rosegg, southern Austria, billeted men in different ways. At Villach, I stayed with a forester, his wife, and their daughter. They were nice people and treated me well. Three long wooden huts were used to billet other men. The dining room and cookhouse were in one hut, and the MT section was in another. The army had to feed civilians, so some patrolmen shot deer in the woods to get food. In nearby Klagenfurt, there was a pretty lake called Wörthersee where the men enjoyed swimming.

My Austrian billet family

There were thoroughbred Hungarian cavalry horses available for our use, as well as army equipment and saddlery. POWs from the German army groomed them.

Popski asked Ben Owen to teach the men how to ride. Ben served in a cavalry unit before joining the Commandos.

There were a number of souvenirs that the men had collected. Fortunately, one of the souvenirs I was wearing was a pair of German jackboots that were one size too large for me. As I bumped painfully along the ground, wondering what to do next, the boot came off and became stuck in the stirrup. I was shaken up and lay on the ground, bruised, but relieved I was still in one piece. The horse was standing nearby, so I put the boot back on, remounted, was more successful second time round, then returned to the stables. A signaller named Jimmy Eastham and a lad called Corkscrew were also learning to ride. Busty, Jimmy's nickname, was also thrown, and Corkscrew, standing nearby, split his sides with laughter. The horse turned around and kicked him in the stomach and he was hospitalized. Knowing how serious an injury like this could be, Ben Owen hurried down there as quickly as possible. He was relieved to find Corkscrew sitting up in bed. However, Ben couldn't control his laughter when he saw

Corkscrew's 'woe is me' expression, and the sister threw him out for laughing at his friend. Ben got bitten by a grass snake that afternoon. Popski forced him back to the hospital, even though he shrugged it off. He had to stay in overnight. The same sister came around with cocoa in the evening. Because she remembered Ben from earlier that day, she wouldn't give him any cocoa.

'I'm going back home then,' said Ben.

'You can't you have been admitted,' she said. Nevertheless, Ben put on his clothes and returned. Next morning, Popski called, 'Bennie!' Ben called back, 'Hello'.

'Come here, I want you,' Popski shouted. Ben went along.

'You have been reported as a deserter at the hospital. I told them you were here. Why did you leave the hospital?'

'They wouldn't give me any cocoa,' answered Ben.

'They would not give you cocoa? Then I don't blame you.' Popski said, as he walked away, smiling.

We had 'acquired' just about every musical instrument ever made. One day, it rained heavily, we put on our capes, picked up instruments such as bugles, trombones, trumpets, etc. Ben Owens' instrument was a large pair of symbols the size of dustbin lids, and we paraded up and down that little street of Rosegg. Nobody could play a note.

Ben Owen. Self Portrait

In their homes, people stared at us through the windows; they must have thought that we were all mad. A little later, in the pub, I performed my version of the current popular songs on the piano without playing a note in tune, of course, and our little group began to sing. As the lads began to think about our loved ones back home, and I thought of my wife, and daughter whom I had never seen, a sort of melancholy descended upon us.

Popski was appointed British Chief Liaison Officer with Russian military forces in Central Europe. For me, Popski was an exceptional man and a hero, and to have been a member of his unit was truly an honour.

Wireless ops, Austria. L to R above. 1st chap, not sure. Stan Steward, Frank Stott, Eric Brooks, Harry Rose, Bottom Row. L to R. Ist chap not sure. Les (Chalky) White, Howard (Toddy) Sloan.

Photo of Hitler taken from a POW.

With a few other wireless operators, I was posted to the Eighth Army Headquarters at Schönbrunn Palace in the third week of August. Schönbrunn in battle-scarred Vienna was the home of the Hapsburgs, a city of music and now hunger, too. We came under the Vienna Occupation Troops. Our billet was located in the rear of the palace, which had been bombed some months before, as you can see in the photo above, and previously occupied by SS troops. Up until civilian personnel took over operations at the palace. We operated wireless links to Whitehall, handled dispatches, and provided security at the

Schönbrunn Palace. 1946. L to R. Mac and Chalky. (Sgmn. Douglas Mc Culloch and Leslie 'Chalky' White)

main gate. I took the dispatches for London to the airdrome situated in the Russian section. The dispatches went by Mosquito plane, and we had to follow a specific route.

One day, my driver, not a PPA man, an employee of the Palace and I, were about half way there, my driver said he was thirsty and needed a drink. I resisted at first but then gave way and we turned into a side street. As we drank our coffee, I glanced toward the café window and noticed several heavily armed Russian guards looking around the jeep. I nudged my driver. 'Look' I said, nodding toward the window. His jaw dropped, and we hurried outside. They pointed their guns at us and asked us, at least it sounded as if they asked us, in Russian, what we were doing there. As neither I nor my driver spoke Russian, they forcibly took us to the Town Hall to be interrogated by their Russian C.O, a ferocious-looking man seated behind a desk.

Angrily hitting his desk with his fist, the C.O. demanded to know what we were doing there. I decided to try German and spoke a few words. For interpretation, he summoned a German-speaking soldier. I explained to him that we go to the airfield every other day and had never stopped at the café before; this was the first time we had taken a break from our journey. The soldier reported this to his C.O., who didn't appear to believe a word of it, and I realized we were in deep trouble. As I clutched the dispatch bag tightly under my arm, I felt uneasy, wishing I had not agreed to stop. Every week, soldiers went missing and were found dead in the canals. As the C.O. stared daggers at us, the airfield was contacted and whilst it seemed a long wait, my explanation was verified.

'You should not leave that road,' the C.O. said angrily through the interpreter. 'We can arrest you because you left it.' Or words to that effect. During this time, my driver stood silently frozen to the spot, and then I heard him whisper nervously in my ear. 'Do you think that he will allow me to smoke a cig?' I posed the question to the interpreter, he posed the question to the C.O., and the C.O. nodded in response.

With hands trembling, my driver offered the C.O. the first cigarette from the packet. A smile spread across the C.O.'s face upon taking one, and the entire atmosphere of the room changed immediately. 'Don't stray off the road again,' the C.O. instructed us. He added, waving us away. 'You are free to leave.' The remainder of the packet of cigarettes was placed on the table by my driver, and we continued our journey to the airdrome.

By the autumn, PPA had been disbanded, and the men had been returned to their original units. Toddy, with whom I had joined the unit, returned to Eighth Army, and I never saw him again. With time, Canadians, Frenchmen, South Africans, a West Indian, Rhodesians, New Zealanders, Russians, and lads from England, Ireland, Scotland and Wales had joined PPA, as well as Major Peniakoff himself, who was Belgian, of Russian descent.

Adolf, an Austrian man about my age, worked at the palace as an interpreter for the British headquarters. Having been drafted into the German army unwillingly, he lost a leg on the Russian front and was then taken to a hospital in Vienna where he recovered. Sgmn. L/Corp. Dougie Mc Culloch 'Mac' of R patrol and I became friends with him and his brother, who also worked at the palace.

When we were off duty, Mac, Adolf and I would visit a beer hall in Vienna. (That is, if Mac was not visiting one of the forester's daughters from my previous billet in Villach). After Russian soldiers confiscated Adolf's father's chandelier factory for a billet for their troops, the factory had gone to the dogs. His father was now trying to restart his business. Several times, I visited his parents, and they were always welcoming to me.

In one instance, Mac, Adolf, and I wandered into the Russian zone without realizing it. We had no indication that we had entered the Russian zone. Upon entering a beer hall, we found it crowded with Russian soldiers; many of them well-oiled with vodka. Seeing the colour drain from Adolf's face, we circled back out pronto.

Popski visited us remaining members of PPA on a regular basis. When he was back with us, he appeared at his happiest. Every week, he arranged a meal at a Vienna restaurant for us. I had the impression that he was trying to hold onto the remaining few, but gradually civilian operators took over the radio links to Whitehall, which allowed me more time to myself, and one by one, the men began receiving news that they would return to their home countries and I, too, was sad to see them leave, as I awaited my turn. In December 1945, Adolf, Mac, and I visited a beer hall around Christmas time. I believe an Austrian priest composed Silent Night, a carol that everyone began singing. As a result of having a few beers, I joined in and sang a verse in German. In a flash, I had a Tommy holding a knife to my throat and shouting, 'Bleedin' Nazi!' There was a brief scuffle before I wrestled the man to the ground. It was luckily amicably resolved in the end. I was invited by Popski to a special reunion party at the Three Hussars restaurant in Vienna, with dancing, buffet, and bar service. Not many of us attended, but it was a memorable evening.

I was informed in January 1946 by an officer in charge of the occupation troops that I was being demobbed, (demobilized). So now it was time to leave the

The evening's menu

army and return to civilian life. I informed Alice of the news in a letter. I said goodbye to Mac and Adolf and promised to keep in touch. Mac decided to remain in the army, and on January 19th, I had a physical and passed fit. The following day, I travelled by rail to Aldershot via Villach. I took only a few 'souvenirs' home with me from the war: signed hotel menus from the patrolmen, some photos and documents, a wanted poster from Tito that I plucked from a tree in Yugoslavia, a prayer book from the Abbot of Assisi Monastery, and a Beretta pistol. Mussolini issued these guns to fascists in order to kill non-fascists. While returning home, I threw the pistol over the side of the boat since I no longer needed it.

Following my return to Aldershot. An officer stamped my release book on 26th January 1946. From this date to 23rd March 1946, release leave was granted with full pay. Overseas leave from 24th March to 30th April 1946, would give me time to find employment. After this date I was transferred to the army reserve. Following my report to the paymaster's office, I sent a telegram to Alice informing her of my expected arrival time on the following day, knowing that the postmistress in Onchan would deliver it to her.

My ration book was given to me along with a small amount of cash, and the following day, I headed to the gymnasium where racks of suits were displayed. The instruction was 'Select a size'. The majority of the suits were navy blue with white pin stripes. One pair of shoes, socks, underwear, shirt and tie; we could keep our army overcoats. With the other lads, I returned to the dormitory to change into civvies and leave our army uniforms on the bed.

With my class A release, I boarded the steamer bound for the Isle of Man on January 27th, 1946. It was a bitterly cold day as we crossed the ocean. I climbed below the deck and lay on a bunk, wondering what sort of employment I should look for now that I am out of the army. During the last six and a half years, I had served as a soldier. I looked at my release certificate: it read Signalman L. R. White. Military conduct, Exemplary. Testimonial: A thoroughly proficient wireless operator, fluent knowledge of German, honest, sober, industrious and careful. Whatever it read, I knew I would take any employment I could find. I stepped off the boat at 6 o'clock.

Outside, it was dark and sleeting. I noticed several people waiting at the pier, but I didn't see Alice. I assumed that she had not received the telegram. Taking a sweeping look at the faces of those present again, I saw her standing alongside Pauline, within the folds of Alice's coat. Pauline hid from me as I approached.

As for Alice, she had hardly changed, but I had. I had not expected to survive the war, and I was aware that I appeared much older. As I embraced her, I was unable to speak because I was overcome with emotion. It has been over two and a half years since I last saw her. As I lifted Pauline up and kissed her, she quickly pulled away from me and began to cry. Alice calmed her by telling her that I was her father, but she clung to Alice tightly.

I took Alice's arm and linked it to mine. 'Darling, let's go home…'

…The End…

Roll Of Honour

Cpl. J. E. Cameron

Tpr. T. Croghan

Sgt. Charles 'Bum' Curtis

Pte. J. Hunter

Lieut. I.W. Mc Callum

Sgmn. D. Mc Culloch

Lt. Mc Gillavray
Lost at sea onboard H.M.S Abdiel. Also, Gunner W.S. Gaskell. No photo available

Sgt. D. J. Porter DCM

Tpr. A. Rogers

Pte. Albert (Chalky) White.

Spr. R. Mc Dowall
No photo available

Cpl. J Snape.
No photo available

Postscript

Les was unable to find employment on the Isle of Man after the war because he was not a Manx national. He and his wife, Alice, settled in England after moving to Manchester.

His Austrian friend Adolf informed Les in May 1946 that Mac, (Douglas Mc Culloch) his fellow PPA colleague and friend, had died after falling under an underground train at Vienna Underground Station. It was believed by many that he had been pushed. He was travelling to Villach to meet his girlfriend.

On November 20th, 2008, Les passed away at the age of ninety, leaving behind three children, eight grandchildren, and twelve great grandchildren.

Acknowledgements

Leslie's army service record
Roy Paterson of F.P.P.A. — Astrolabe publishers FPPA. Website. PPA War diaries
Angela Brooks, daughter of Eric–for providing the photos on page 128 and 129
Kurt – PPA Preservation Society. Belgium.
http://userspandora.be/ppa
Ben Owen

Internet websites and other sources
Leslie's WW2 PPA letters home, and DVD discs, placed with POPSKI'S PRIVATE ARMY collection Imperial War Museum. London and the Signals Museum, Blatchford.

Though every effort has been made to verify facts and information, I sincerely hope that any omissions or errors will not cause offence to families, friends, or associations.
I dedicate this book to my late father-in-law and co-author, Leslie. I would also like to thank several family members for their encouragement.

Anne Whyte.

Printed in Dunstable, United Kingdom